The Daily Office

A Simple Guide to Morning and Evening Prayer

Drawing from Scripture,
the Book of Common Prayer,
and Other Sources

Compiled and edited by Aaron Sandford and Jacob Young
Designed by Aaron Sandford

Essays and design © 2023 by Aaron Sandford.
ISBN-13: 979-8-218-18341-7

The majority of the content of this book is from the 1979 edition of The Book of Common Prayer, which is in the public domain. Some additional content has been taken from the 1928 edition, also in the public domain.

Scripture quotations are from The ESV® Bible (The Holy Bible, English Standard Version®), copyright © 2001 by Crossway, a publishing ministry of Good News Publishers. Used by permission. All rights reserved.

This book is designed using typefaces from the Corundum font family. Most photography was sourced from unsplash.com.

Published by Sandford Design LLC
Cincinnati, Ohio

Printed in the United States of America.

Contents

Introduction 5

Morning Office 11

Evening Office 27

Morning Short Prayer 43

Evening Short Prayer 53

Appendices 63
    Lectionary 64
    Psalter 88
    Readings for Holy Days Whose Dates Vary 89
    Collects for Holy Days 90
    Lenten Praise 101

"Praying Hands" by Albrecht Dürer (Public Domain)

Introduction

Sometimes the best words to express what you want or need to say have already been put together.

Several years ago, looking for a way to enrich my devotional life, I came across the concept of the Daily Office and was intrigued. Prayer at that time felt confused and unstructured, and my heart resonated with the idea of a long tradition of words filled with beauty and truth that I could hitch my faith to and let form the path of my thoughts.

But how to start? Books I read convinced me I was interested in practicing the Office but gave me little guidance in starting. The Book of Common Prayer (BCP) itself seemed complicated, overwhelming. The series of booklets (based on the BCP) that I would eventually use, from the non-profit Anglican Compass, confused me enough with its instructions to skip around and make choices that it would be several years before I actually began to use it.

But after I did use it, I grew to love it. I loved the liturgy of it that shepherded my focus through worship, confession, gratitude, and supplication. I loved that it made my routine more predictable. I loved that it framed my day with beauty, and that both the precise words and general themes of the prayers got etched into my memory.

So when Anglican Compass took a break from producing their periodical Daily Office booklets, and having heard a few friends express interest in a more rich and guided prayer life, I attempted to apply my expertise in design and UX to make one perennial design you could follow straight through, shortening the learning curve and slightly customizing the structure to be more friendly to solitary prayer.

I am by no means an expert here. But that is the beauty of the Office: It's the expert for you. It's nearly as old as Christianity in English, the first version predating the publication of the King James Bible by 62 years. It contains a mix of carefully chosen Scripture passages and beautiful prayers full of realism, hope, and wonder. It is inherently communal, both in the sense that it is meant to be prayed with a group and in the sense that believers around the world are praying the same prayers.

The word "office" itself comes from the Latin officium divinum, "divine service"—the work of the collective people of God.

How This Works

So how do you get started?

I've tried to get rid of guesswork, so hopefully it's no more complicated than opening up to a prayer section and diving in. That said, you should feel free to use the book as a resource in whatever way you find most helpful and life-giving.

The prayers are divided into four sections: (1) morning and (2) evening Offices, and (3) morning and (4) evening Short Prayers.

In a sense, the Offices are the "full experience"—rich and comprehensive. While not lengthy, they do add up: each Office takes a good 12 to 15 minutes without scriptural and/or devotional readings, and readings can add five minutes to half an hour or more. A full morning-and-evening practice can easily take up an hour each day. If you have kids, are new to devotional disciplines, or have a busy schedule, that might seem daunting.

That's where the Short Prayers come in. Taken from the Book of Common Prayer like the Offices, these prayers make setting aside time for formal prayers more accessible for those with limited time and provide a great structure for family devotions.

Regardless of which prayers you are praying—Short or Office, morning or evening—the actual how-to is the same: Start at the beginning and read your way through, following the directions (or modifying them to what works best for you).

A few practical ideas:

- Don't bite off more than you can chew. If you're not sure you'll have time, start with the Short Prayers, or start with just one morning or evening practice.

- Remember that these are prayers: offer them to God. There is an element of reciting, but recite them as meaningful words addressed to a listening God and with your faith and will attached.

- On the other hand, don't hesitate to move quickly. The preparers of the Office have poured their effort into knowing what to say to God, and you don't need to reinvent the wheel. Move through the prayers meditatively when it's life-giving, but one of the ways that I personally have benefited from the Daily Office is escaping what I might call "foggy prayer": the sort of unmoored internal monologue in which futile grasping for the right words made prayer little more than feeling confused and frustrated before God. The Office was freeing because it had figured out what to say. I just had to go ahead and say it.

- I like to keep three bookmarks in this book: one for morning prayer, one for evening prayer, and one for the lectionary.

- Regularity is more important than passion. I'm preaching to myself here—as I write, this is something I'm struggling with—but I have found the office to be most impactful when I was using it morning and evening with attention and regularity but without high expectations (of either the experience or of myself) and seldom with spark, much less fire. Showing up and simply praying through quickly but with focus made a difference for the richness and joy of my life. We're after embers, not crackling pine needles.

Regarding the design of the prayers for group practice: I have tried to optimize this book for individual use since that's the most common use case for me and, I expect, for many others. If you have the chance to pray as a group, though, the Office can provide a beautiful structure. Praying with a few people, I might consider taking turns reading prayers. With a larger group, or for a more traditional approach, you might look up the prayers in the actual Book of Common Prayer (available online for free as well as in print) and follow its guidance on which parts are to be read by an officiant/leader and which are said collectively by the people.

THOUGHTS ON PHYSICAL WORSHIP

Why stand, kneel, and make the sign of the cross? Aren't those empty formalities? Roman Catholic?

To answer the first two questions: At least part of the intention behind all of these physical practices is to remind us that we are whole beings—body, mind, spirit, emotions, all integral parts of being human and created in God's image—serving a God who created us physical. These actions are opportunities to pray with our bodies as well as with our words.

This, by the way, could also be considered a reason to pray aloud. The thirteenth-century theologian Thomas Aquinas wrote in his *Summa Theologica* that while praying aloud is not necessary and is even inadvisable if it distracts, it is generally good because [a] it helps to focus the mind, [b] it is an act of service to God to use our whole selves in prayer and worship, and [c] when our heart is full, speech is a natural overflow of feeling into the body (ST II-II, 83, xii). All three points, but especially the second, might also be true of other physical demonstrations.

Briefly, kneeling is an act of submission. Standing is an act of reverence and often proclamation. The sign of the cross is an act of marking oneself set apart for, and of belief in, the Triune God.

As to the connection to Roman Catholicism: kneeling, standing, and the sign of the cross have all historically been practiced since the early days of the church. Kneeling for prayer is described in the Bible in both the Old and New Testaments. Standing for Scripture readings has some biblical roots as well. The sign of the cross is a bit less ancient, but a version of it is described by the early church father Tertullian as early as the third century (before the Roman church claimed universal authority based on succession of its bishop from Peter).

For the sake of those who might find making the sign of the cross uncomfortable, I have indicated where to perform that gesture with a cross symbol (technically a dagger glyph): †. If you do not wish to perform that gesture, you might use the symbol as a *visual* reminder of the same things that the sign of the cross is a *physical* reminder of.

Much of the work done for this book is inspired by previous work done by the non-profit Anglican Compass, which hosts a blog that has some more useful thoughts on some of these topics, including the following posts:

https://anglicancompass.com/why-do-we-kneel-in-prayer/

http://anglicancompass.com/the-sign-of-the-cross/

Sources, Resources, and Thanks

The prayers here largely come from the 1979 and 1928 editions of the BCP. Many of the prayers have been lightly edited, mostly to modernize language (turning "thees" to "yous") and in a few rare cases making more substantial adjustments (e.g., removing "the power of" from "conceived by the power of the Holy Spirit" in the Apostle's Creed, which reflects earlier versions of the creed; or adding "apart from your grace" to the "there is no health in us" in the Morning Office confession). Any prayer that is changed even slightly from its cited source is marked with a dougle dagger (‡) in the citation.

Other departures from the prayers as curated in the BCP: Prayers and passages taken directly from Scripture are rendered in the English Standard Version. I have included a few additional passages that I have found helpful for daily reflection. One or two prayers have been dropped, a couple "occasional prayers" from elsewhere in the BCP added, and what would be the second confession of the day has been replaced with a simple prayer of examen, a traditional Jesuit prayer of self-examination in the presence of a merciful and available God.

Anglican Compass's blog includes a wealth of posts answering all kinds of Daily Office-related questions, and they produce periodical Daily Office booklets downloadable from their website at anglicancompass.com/dailyofficebooklet.

The site dailyoffice2019.com includes midday and bedtime prayers and spells out the readings.

Various versions of the BCP, including the 1979 and the Anglican Church in North America's 2019 edition, can be found online for free.

Robert Benson's *In Constant Prayer* poetically explores the beauty and worth of the Daily Office. I found it compelling and motivating (though not instructive).

I am very grateful for the help of my friend and former pastor, Jacob Young, who encouraged this project, provided loads of useful feedback that shaped both content and format, and helped compile and edit the prayers from the BCP. I also want to thank my friend Peter Denio, who served as a mentor during the crucial time when I was beginning to seek out practices that would ground and enrich my faith. He generously shared his own practices of prayer and spiritual disciplines with me and loaned me books that he rightly thought might be useful, and he also provided encouraging feedback when I shared a copy of this work with him.

    I hope this book is useful to anyone desiring a historically grounded and formative prayer practice, novice or veteran, and I welcome any feedback on what aspects of the format and content are helpful and what the learning curve is like if you're new to the Office.

—   Aaron Sandford
         December 2022
         dailyoffice@sandford.design

Morning Office

Photo by Maurício Guardiano

PREPARE

PRAY FOR THE SPIRIT OF PRAYER

1979 Book of Common Prayer‡

O Almighty God, You who pour out on all who desire it the spirit of grace and of supplication:

Deliver us, when we draw near to you, from coldness of heart and wanderings of mind, that with steadfast thoughts and kindled affections we may worship you in spirit and in truth; through Jesus Christ our Lord.

QUIET YOUR SOUL BEFORE GOD

KEEP SILENCE FOR SEVERAL MINUTES.

Consider this a time of wordless prayer. If your mind is full of distraction, pray one of these simple prayers repeatedly.

- Jesus.
- Jesus Christ, Son of God, have mercy on me, a sinner.
- Jesus, I am safe with you.
- Jesus is enough.
- Lord, I am here with you, and you are here with me.
- Behold the Lamb of God, who takes away the sin of the world.

It may be helpful to predetermine the amount of time to be spent in silence and use a timer.

Confess

Humbly Confess Your Need for God—His Forgiveness, Healing, and Sanctifying Work.

1979 Book of Common Prayer‡

Kneel.

For a short time, a minute or so at most, examine your conscience. Acknowledge any specific sins for which to ask forgiveness, or weaknesses for which you need the Lord's help.

Almighty and most merciful Father, we have erred and strayed from your ways like lost sheep, we have followed too much the devices and desires of our own hearts, we have offended against your holy laws, we have left undone those things which we ought to have done, and we have done those things which we ought not to have done, and we have no health in us apart from your grace.

But you, O Lord, have mercy upon us, spare those who confess their faults, restore those who are penitent, according to your promises declared unto mankind in Christ Jesus our Lord; and grant, O most merciful Father, for his sake, that we may hereafter live a godly, righteous, and sober life, to the glory of your holy Name.

Amen.

Grant to your faithful people pardon and peace, that we may be cleansed from all our sins, and serve you with a quiet mind.

Amen.

Rise.

Praise the Creator

During Lent, pray instead the Benedictus Es, Domine, on page 101

Pray the Te Deum

1928 Book of Common Prayer‡

We praise you, O God; we confess that you are Lord. All the earth worships you, the Father everlasting. To you all angels cry aloud, and all the heavenly powers. To you, Cherubim and Seraphim continually cry: Holy, Holy, Holy, Lord God of Hosts; heaven and earth are full of the majesty of your glory. The glorious company of the apostles praise you. The goodly fellowship of the prophets praise you. The noble army of martyrs praise you. The holy Church throughout all the world acclaims you: Father, of majesty unbounded, your true and only Son, worthy of all worship, and the Holy Spirit, advocate and guide.

You are the King of Glory, O Christ. You are the everlasting Son of the Father. When you became man to set us free you did not shun the Virgin's womb. When you overcame the sharpness of death, you opened the Kingdom of Heaven to all believers. You sit at the right hand of God, in the glory of the Father. We believe that you will come to be our Judge. Come then, Lord, and help your servants, bought with the price of your own blood, and number us with your saints in glory everlasting.

O Lord, save your people, and bless your inheritance. Govern them and lift them up for ever. Day by day we magnify you; we praise your Name forever.

Grant, O Lord, to keep us this day without sin. O Lord, have mercy upon us, have mercy upon us. O Lord, let your mercy be upon us, for our trust is in you. O Lord, in you have I trusted; let me never be put to shame.

Learn

Pray for a Receptive Heart

1928 Book of Common Prayer‡

Blessed Lord, you caused all holy Scriptures to be written for our learning; grant that we may hear them, read, mark, learn, and inwardly digest them in such a way that by patience and the comfort of your holy Word we may embrace and securely grasp the blessed hope of everlasting life, which you have given us in our Savior Jesus Christ. Amen.

Spend some time in scripture.

This can also be a time for learning through devotional readings if scripture has already or will be read that day. The Daily Office Lectionary Readings are included on page 64 and can be followed in a one-year or two-year reading plan, but any reading plan can be used here. When pressed for time, a Psalm is a good option, and a reading plan for all the Psalms in a month is included on page 88.

Celebrate the Faithfulness of God

Pray the Benedictus

Zechariah rejoices over John the Baptist
Luke 1: 68-79, ESV

Blessed be the Lord God of Israel, for he has visited and redeemed his people and has raised up a horn of salvation for us in the house of his servant David, as he spoke by the mouth of his holy prophets from of old, that we should be saved from our enemies and from the hand of all who hate us; to show the mercy promised to our fathers and to remember his holy covenant, the oath that he swore to our father Abraham, to grant us that we, being delivered from the hand of our enemies, might serve him without fear, in holiness and righteousness before him all our days.

And you, child*, will be called the prophet of the Most High; for you will go before the Lord to prepare his ways, to give knowledge of salvation to his people in the forgiveness of their sins, because of the tender mercy of our God, whereby the sunrise shall visit us from on high to give light to those who sit in darkness and in the shadow of death, to guide our feet into the way of peace.

†

Glory be to the Father,
and to the Son,
and to the Holy Spirit;
as it was in the beginning, is now,
and ever shall be, world without
end. Amen.

---

* The "child" Zechariah addresses in this verse of his song of praise to God is the newborn John the Baptist, the herald of the soon-to-be-born Messiah.

Affirm the Faith

Recite the Apostles' Creed

1979 Book of Common Prayer‡

Stand.

I believe in God, the Father almighty, creator of heaven and earth.

I believe in Jesus Christ, his only Son, our Lord. He was conceived by the Holy Spirit and born of the Virgin Mary. He suffered under Pontius Pilate, was crucified, died, and was buried. He descended to the dead. On the third day he rose again. He ascended into heaven, and is seated at the right hand of the Father. He will come again to judge the living and the dead.

I believe in the Holy Spirit, the holy catholic Church, the communion of saints, the forgiveness of sins, the resurrection of the body, and the life everlasting. Amen.

Pray as Jesus Taught

Pray the Lord's Prayer

1979 Book of Common Prayer; Mt. 6:9–13

Kneel.

Our Father, who art in heaven, hallowed be Thy name.

Thy Kingdom come, Thy will be done, on earth as it is in heaven.

Give us this day our daily bread;

And forgive us our trespasses as we forgive those who trespass against us.

And lead us not into temptation, but deliver us from evil.

For Thine is the Kingdom, the power, and the glory for ever and ever. Amen.

Rise.

Seek God's Mercy

Pray the Suffrages

1979 Book of Common Prayer‡

Show us your mercy, O Lord, and grant us your salvation.

Clothe your ministers with righteousness; let your people sing with joy.

Give peace, O Lord, in all the world, for only in you can we live in safety.

Lord, keep this nation under your care, and guide us in the way of justice and truth.

Let your way be known upon earth, your saving health among all nations.

Let not the needy, O Lord, be forgotten, nor the hope of the poor be taken away.

Create in us clean hearts, O God, and take not your Holy Spirit from us.

Advance the Gospel

A Prayer for Mission

1979 Book of Common Prayer

Lord Jesus Christ, you stretched out your arms of love on the hard wood of the Cross that everyone might come within the reach of your saving embrace: So clothe us in your Spirit that we, reaching forth our hands in love, may bring those who do not know you to the knowledge and love of you; for the honor of your Name.

Amen.

Pray the Daily Collect

"A collect is simply a prayer meant to gather the intentions of the people and the focus of worship into a succinct prayer." —Anglican Compass

Feast days and other holy days have specific collects to replace these daily collects. Special collects are included on page 90. The Lectionary tables starting on page 64 will tell you if it is a holy day.

All daily collects are taken from the 1979 Book of Common Prayer except the Wednesday prayer, which is adapted from the 1928 Book of Common Prayer.

Sunday

A Collect for Strength to Await Christ's Return

O God our King, by the resurrection of your Son Jesus Christ on the first day of the week, you conquered sin, put death to flight, and gave us the hope of everlasting life: Redeem all our days by this victory; forgive our sins, banish our fears, make us bold to praise you and to do your will; and steel us to wait for the consummation of your kingdom on the last great Day; through the same Jesus Christ our Lord. Amen.

Monday

A Collect for Renewal of Life

O God, the King eternal, whose light divides the day from the night and turns the shadow of death into the morning: Drive far from us all wrong desires, incline our hearts to keep your law, and guide our feet into the way of peace; that, having done your will with cheerfulness during the day, we may, when night comes, rejoice to give you thanks; through Jesus Christ our Lord. Amen.

Tuesday

A Collect for Peace

O God, the author of peace and lover of concord, to know you is eternal life and to serve you is perfect freedom: Defend us, your humble servants, in all assaults of our enemies; that we, surely trusting in your defense, may not fear the power of any adversaries; through the might of Jesus Christ our Lord. Amen.

Wednesday

A Collect for Grace

O LORD, our heavenly Father, Almighty and everlasting God, you have safely brought us to the beginning of this day; Defend us today with your mighty power, and grant that we might neither fall into sin nor run into any kind of danger; but sovereignly order all we do that it might be righteous in your sight; through Jesus Christ our Lord. Amen.

Thursday

A Collect for Guidance

Heavenly Father, in you we live and move and have our being: We humbly pray you so to guide and govern us by your Holy Spirit, that in all the cares and occupations of our life we may not forget you, but may remember that we are ever walking in your sight; through Jesus Christ our Lord. Amen.

Friday

A Collect for Endurance

Almighty God, whose most dear Son went not up to joy but first he suffered pain, and entered not into glory before he was crucified: Mercifully grant that we, walking in the way of the cross, may find it none other than the way of life and peace; through Jesus Christ your Son our Lord. Amen.

Saturday

A Collect for Sabbath Rest

Almighty God, who after the creation of the world rested from all your works and sanctified a day of rest for all your creatures: Grant that we, putting away all earthly anxieties, may be duly prepared for the service of your sanctuary, and that our rest here upon earth may be a preparation for the eternal rest promised to your people in heaven; through Jesus Christ our Lord. Amen.

Turn Your Heart toward Beauty

Direct Your Mind

From Philippians 4, ESV

Whatever is true,
whatever is honorable,
whatever is just,
whatever is pure,
whatever is lovely,
whatever is commendable,
if there is any excellence,
if there is anything worthy of
praise, think about these things.

Orient Your Desire

From Galatians 5, ESV

The fruit of the Spirit is
love,
joy,
peace,
patience,
kindness,
goodness,
faithfulness,
gentleness,
self-control.

OFFER PETITIONS, INTERCESSIONS, AND THANKS

DON'T LET YOURSELF GET BOGGED DOWN. GOD KNOWS WHAT IS NEEDED. HE WANTS TO HEAR YOU, BUT IF YOU DON'T KNOW WHAT TO SAY, OR IF YOU ARE PRESSED FOR TIME, SIMPLY BRING NEEDS BEFORE GOD AND FOLLOW THIS FORMAT:

FOR _____: LORD, HAVE MERCY. CHRIST, HAVE MERCY.

OFFER GRATITUDE FOR AT LEAST 3 THINGS

LIST REPEATED PRAYERS

Family, friends, enemies, the suffering, desires, fears, needs, the culture, the world

If you are following the evening office and/or other times of prayer as well, divide your list among prayer times however seems wise and fits your schedule.

PRAY FOR THOSE WHO COME TO MIND

Give Thanks to God

The General Thanksgiving and the Grace.

1979 Book of Common Prayer

Almighty God, Father of all mercies: we your unworthy servants give you humble thanks for all your goodness and loving-kindness to us and to all whom you have made.

We bless you for our creation, preservation, and all the blessings of this life—but above all for your immeasurable love in the redemption of the world by our Lord Jesus Christ; for the means of grace, and for the hope of glory.

And, we pray, give us such an awareness of your mercies, that with truly thankful hearts we may show forth your praise, not only with our lips, but in our lives, by giving up our selves to your service and by walking before you in holiness and righteousness all our days; through Jesus Christ our Lord, to whom, with you and the Holy Spirit, be honor and glory throughout all ages. Amen.

✝

The grace of our Lord Jesus Christ, and the love of God, and the fellowship of the Holy Spirit, be with us all evermore. Amen.

Photo by Robin Schreiner

Evening Office

Photo by Lisa Adams

PREPARE

PREPARE FOR PERSONAL PRAYER

1979 Book of Common Prayer

Almighty, everlasting God, let our prayer in your sight be as incense, the lifting up of our hands as the evening sacrifice. Give us grace to behold you, present in your Word and Sacraments, and to recognize you in the lives of those around us. Stir up in us the flame of that love which burned in the heart of your Son as he bore his passion, and let it burn in us to eternal life and to the ages of ages. Amen.

PRACTICE THE PRESENCE OF GOD

KEEP SILENCE FOR SEVERAL MINUTES.

Consider this a time of wordless prayer. If your mind is full of distraction, pray one of these simple prayers repeatedly.

- Jesus.
- Jesus Christ, Son of God, have mercy on me, a sinner.
- Jesus, I am safe with you.
- Jesus is enough.
- Lord, I am here with you, and you are here with me.
- Behold the Lamb of God, who takes away the sin of the world.

It may be helpful to predetermine the amount of time to be spent in silence and use a timer.

Examine

Review your day with gratitude and repentance.

Thank God for three things you're grateful for from the day.

Reflect for one or two minutes on your day—what went well? What went poorly? What emotions did you feel?

Bring your reflections to God and ask for His guidance and forgiveness for your failures.

Rest in God's Guidance and Forgiveness

1979 Book of Common Prayer; cf. Ps. 31:5, 17:8

Into your hands, O Lord,
I commend my spirit,
for you have redeemed me, O Lord,
O God of truth.

Keep us, O Lord,
as the apple of your eye;
hide us under the shadow
of your wings.

Lord, have mercy.
Christ, have mercy.
Lord, have mercy.

From Isaiah 30:15:

Thus said the Lord God, the Holy One of Israel, "In returning and rest you shall be saved; in quietness and in trust shall be your strength."

Praise the Creator

Pray the Phos Hilaron
1979 Book of Common Prayer‡

O gladdening Light, pure brightness of the everliving Father in heaven,

O Jesus Christ, holy and blessed!

Now as we come to the setting of the sun, and our eyes behold the vesper light, we sing your praises, O God:

Father,
Son, and
Holy Spirit.

You are worthy at all times to be praised by happy voices, O Son of God, O Giver of Life, and to be glorified through all the worlds.

Learn

Pray for Inner Renewal
Adapted from 2 Tim. 3:16-17, Romans 15:4

O God, you breathed out all of Scripture and gave it to us for nourishment, to encourage us and give us hope. As we turn now to Your Word, open our hearts to profit from its teaching, reproof, correction, and training in righteousness, that we may be complete and equipped for every good work. Amen.

Spend some time in scripture.

This can also be a time for learning through devotional readings if scripture has already or will be read that day. The Daily Office Lectionary Readings are included on page 64 and can be followed in a one-year or two-year reading plan, but any reading plan can be used here. When pressed for time, a Psalm is a good option, and a reading plan for all the Psalms in a month is included on page 88.

Celebrate the Faithfulness of God

Pray the Magnificat

The Song of Mary
Luke 1:46-55, ESV

My soul magnifies the Lord, and my spirit rejoices in God my Savior; for he has regarded the lowliness of his handmaiden.

For behold, from now on, all generations will call me blessed; for he that is mighty has magnified me, and holy is his Name.

And his mercy is on those who fear him, throughout all generations.

He has shown the strength of his arm; he has scattered the proud in the imagination of their hearts. He has brought down the mighty from their thrones, and has exalted the humble and meek. He has filled the hungry with good things, and the rich he has sent empty away.

He, remembering his mercy, has helped his servant Israel, as he promised to our fathers, Abraham and his seed for ever.

✝

Glory be to the Father, and to the Son, and to the Holy Spirit; as it was in the beginning, is now, and ever shall be, world without end.

Amen.

Affirm the Faith

Recite the Nicene Creed

1979 Book of Common Prayer

Stand.

We believe in one God, the Father, the Almighty, maker of heaven and earth, of all that is, seen and unseen.

We believe in one Lord, Jesus Christ, the only Son of God, eternally begotten of the Father, God from God, Light from Light, true God from true God, begotten, not made, of one Being with the Father. Through him all things were made. For us and for our salvation he came down from heaven: by the power of the Holy Spirit he became incarnate from the Virgin Mary, and was made man. For our sake he was crucified under Pontius Pilate; he suffered death and was buried.

On the third day he rose again in accordance with the Scriptures; he ascended into heaven and is seated at the right hand of the Father. He will come again in glory to judge the living and the dead, and his kingdom will have no end.

We believe in the Holy Spirit, the Lord, the giver of life, who proceeds from the Father and the Son. With the Father and the Son he is worshiped and glorified. He has spoken through the Prophets. We believe in one holy catholic and apostolic Church. We acknowledge one baptism for the forgiveness of sins. We look for the resurrection of the dead, and the life of the world to come.

Amen.

Pray as Jesus Taught

Pray the Lord's Prayer

1979 Book of Common Prayer; Mt. 6:9–13

Kneel.

Our Father, who art in heaven, hallowed be Thy name.

Thy Kingdom come, Thy will be done, on earth as it is in heaven.

Give us this day our daily bread;

And forgive us our trespasses as we forgive those who trespass against us.

And lead us not into temptation, but deliver us from evil.

For Thine is the Kingdom, the power, and the glory for ever and ever. Amen.

Rise.

Seek God's Mercy

Pray the Entreaties

1979 Book of Common Prayer

That this evening may be holy, good, and peaceful,
> We entreat you, O Lord.

That your holy angels may lead us in paths of peace and goodwill,
> We entreat you, O Lord.

That we may be pardoned and forgiven for our sins and offenses,
> We entreat you, O Lord.

That there may be peace to your Church and to the whole world,
> We entreat you, O Lord.

That we may depart this life in your faith and fear, and not be condemned before the great judgment seat of Christ,
> We entreat you, O Lord.

That we may be bound together by your Holy Spirit in the communion of all your saints, entrusting one another and all our life to Christ,
> We entreat you, O Lord.

Pray the Daily Collect

"A collect is simply a prayer meant to gather the intentions of the people and the focus of worship into a succinct prayer." —Anglican Compass

Feast days and other holy days have specific collects to replace these daily collects. Special collects are included on page 90. The Lectionary tables starting on page 64 will tell you if it is a holy day.

All daily collects are taken from the 1979 Book of Common Prayer.

Sunday

A Collect for Resurrection Hope

Lord God, whose Son our Savior Jesus Christ triumphed over the powers of death and prepared for us our place in the new Jerusalem: Grant that we, who have this day given thanks for his resurrection, may praise you in that City of which he is the light, and where he lives and reigns for ever and ever. Amen.

Monday

A Collect for Peace

Most holy God, the source of all good desires, all right judgments, and all just works: Give to us, your servants, that peace which the world cannot give, so that our minds may be fixed on the doing of your will, and that we, being delivered from the fear of all enemies, may live in peace and quietness; through the mercies of Christ Jesus our Savior. Amen.

Tuesday

A Collect for Presence and Aid

Keep watch, dear Lord, with those who work, or watch, or weep this night, and give your angels charge over those who sleep. Tend the sick, Lord Christ; give rest to the weary, bless the dying, soothe the suffering, pity the afflicted, shield the joyous; and all for your love's sake. Amen.

Wednesday

A Collect for Protection

O God, the life of all who live, the light of the faithful, the strength of those who labor, and the repose of the dead: We thank you for the blessings of the day that is past, and humbly ask for your protection through the coming night. Bring us in safety to the morning hours; through him who died and rose again for us, your Son our Savior Jesus Christ. Amen.

Thursday

A Collect for the Presence of Christ

Lord Jesus, stay with us, for evening is at hand and the day is past; be our companion in the way, kindle our hearts, and awaken hope, that we may know you as you are revealed in Scripture and the breaking of bread. Grant this for the sake of your love. Amen.

Friday

A Collect for Faith

Lord Jesus Christ, by your death you took away the sting of death: Grant to us your servants so to follow in faith where you have led the way, that we may at length fall asleep peacefully in you and wake up in your likeness; for your tender mercies' sake. Amen.

Saturday

A Collect for the Eve of Worship

O God, the source of eternal light: Shed forth your unending day upon us who watch for you, that our lips may praise you, our lives may bless you, and our worship on the morrow give you glory; through Jesus Christ our Lord. Amen.

Turn Your Heart toward Beauty

Contemplate Love

From 1 Corinthians 13 and 1 John 4

If I give away all I have, and if I deliver up my body to be burned, but have not love, I gain nothing.

Love is patient and kind; love does not envy or boast; it is not arrogant or rude.

It does not insist on its own way; it is not irritable or resentful; it does not rejoice at wrongdoing, but rejoices with the truth.

Love bears all things, believes all things, hopes all things, endures all things. Love never ends.

Beloved, let us love one another, for love is from God, and whoever loves has been born of God and knows God. Anyone who does not love does not know God, because God is love.

Offer Petitions, Intercessions, and Thanks

Don't let yourself get bogged down. God knows what is needed. He wants to hear you, but if you don't know what to say, or if you are pressed for time, simply bring needs before God and follow this format:

For _____: Lord, have mercy. Christ, have mercy.

List Repeated Prayers

Family, friends, enemies, the suffering, desires, fears, needs, the culture, the world

If you are following the evening office and/or other times of prayer as well, divide your list among prayer times however seems wise and fits your schedule.

Pray for Those Who Come to Mind

Give Thanks to God

The General Thanksgiving and a Benediction.

1979 Book of Common Prayer

Almighty God, Father of all mercies: we your unworthy servants give you humble thanks for all your goodness and loving-kindness to us and to all whom you have made.

We bless you for our creation, preservation, and all the blessings of this life—but above all for your immeasurable love in the redemption of the world by our Lord Jesus Christ; for the means of grace, and for the hope of glory.

And, we pray, give us such an awareness of your mercies, that with truly thankful hearts we may show forth your praise, not only with our lips, but in our lives, by giving up our selves to your service and by walking before you in holiness and righteousness all our days;

✝

through Jesus Christ our Lord, to whom, with you and the Holy Spirit, be honor and glory throughout all ages. Amen.

—

May the God of hope fill us with all joy and peace in believing through the power of the Holy Spirit.

Amen.

Photo by Michael Krahn

Morning Short Prayer

Photo by Czapp Botond

Come Before God

Ask for God's Help to Pray

Psalm 51:15

O Lord, open my lips, and my mouth shall show forth your praise.

Confess Your Need for Mercy and Turn Toward God's Help

1979 Book of Common Prayer

Most merciful God, we confess that we have sinned against you in thought, word, and deed, by what we have done, and by what we have left undone. We have not loved you with our whole heart; we have not loved our neighbors as ourselves. We are truly sorry and we humbly repent. For the sake of your Son Jesus Christ, have mercy on us and forgive us; that we may delight in your will, and walk in your ways, to the glory of your Name. Amen.

†

Glory be to the Father,
and to the Son,
and to the Holy Spirit;
as it was in the beginning, is now, and ever shall be, world without end. Amen.

Learn

Read the passage of the day or follow another reading plan. Devotional lessons from other sources than the Bible can also be read at this time. For other reading plans, see the Lectionary on page 64 and the Psalter on page 88.

Sunday

Blessed be the God and Father of our Lord Jesus Christ! According to his great mercy, he has caused us to be born again to a living hope through the resurrection of Jesus Christ from the dead.

1 Peter 1:3

Monday

Give thanks to the Father, who has qualified you to share in the inheritance of the saints in light. He has delivered us from the domain of darkness and transferred us to the kingdom of his beloved Son, in whom we have redemption, the forgiveness of sins.

Colossians 1:12-14

Tuesday

If then you have been raised with Christ, seek the things that are above, where Christ is, seated at the right hand of God. Set your minds on things that are above, not on things that are on earth. For you have died, and your life is hidden with Christ in God. When Christ who is your life appears, then you also will appear with him in glory.

Colossians 3:1-4

Wednesday

Abide in me, and I in you. As the branch cannot bear fruit by itself, unless it abides in the vine, neither can you, unless you abide in me. I am the vine; you are the branches. Whoever abides in me and I in him, he it is that bears much fruit, for apart from me you can do nothing.

John 15:4-5

Thursday

Do not be anxious about anything, but in everything by prayer and supplication with thanksgiving let your requests be made known to God. And the peace of God, which surpasses all understanding, will guard your hearts and your minds in Christ Jesus.

Philippians 4:6-7

Friday

Since then we have a great high priest who has passed through the heavens, Jesus, the Son of God, let us hold fast our confession. For we do not have a high priest who is unable to sympathize with our weaknesses, but one who in every respect has been tempted as we are, yet without sin. Let us then with confidence draw near to the throne of grace, that we may receive mercy and find grace to help in time of need.

Hebrews 4:14-16

Saturday

The LORD is gracious and merciful, slow to anger and abounding in steadfast love. The LORD is good to all, and his mercy is over all that he has made.

Psalm 145:8-9

Keep Silence

Quiet Your Soul before God

Keep silence for one minute.

Consider this a time of wordless prayer. If your mind is full of distraction, pray one of these simple prayers repeatedly.

- *Jesus.*
- *Jesus Christ, Son of God, have mercy on me, a sinner.*
- *Jesus, I am safe with you.*
- *Jesus is enough.*
- *Lord, I am here with you, and you are here with me.*
- *Behold the Lamb of God, who takes away the sin of the world.*

It may be helpful to predetermine the amount of time to be spent in silence and use a timer.

Affirm the Faith

Recite the Apostles' Creed or Sing a Hymn

1979 Book of Common Prayer‡

Stand.

I believe in God, the Father almighty, creator of heaven and earth.

I believe in Jesus Christ, his only Son, our Lord. He was conceived by the Holy Spirit and born of the Virgin Mary. He suffered under Pontius Pilate, was crucified, died, and was buried. He descended to the dead. On the third day he rose again. He ascended into heaven, and is seated at the right hand of the Father. He will come again to judge the living and the dead.

I believe in the Holy Spirit, the holy catholic Church, the communion of saints, the forgiveness of sins, the resurrection of the body, and the life everlasting. Amen.

Offer Petitions, Intercessions, and Thanks

Pray as Jesus Taught

Feel free to simply bring needs before God and follow this format:

For _____:
Lord, have mercy. Christ, have mercy.

Offer Gratitude for 3 Things

Keep a List of Repeated Prayers

Family, friends, enemies, the suffering, desires, fears, needs, the culture, the world

If you are following the evening office and/or other times of prayer as well, divide your list among prayer times however seems wise and fits your schedule.

Pray for Those Who Come to Mind

Pray the Lord's Prayer

1979 Book of Common Prayer; Mt. 6:9–13

Kneel.

Our Father, who art in heaven, hallowed be Thy name.

Thy Kingdom come, Thy will be done, on earth as it is in heaven.

Give us this day our daily bread;

And forgive us our trespasses as we forgive those who trespass against us.

And lead us not into temptation, but deliver us from evil.

For Thine is the Kingdom, the power, and the glory for ever and ever. Amen.

Rise.

Pray the Collect

A Collect for Grace

1979 Book of Common Prayer

Lord God, almighty and everlasting Father, you have brought us in safety to this new day: Preserve us with your mighty power, that we may not fall into sin, nor be overcome by adversity; and in all we do, direct us to the fulfilling of your purpose; through Jesus Christ our Lord. Amen.

✝

The grace of our Lord Jesus Christ, and the love of God, and the fellowship of the Holy Spirit, be with us all evermore. Amen.

Photo by Tomasz Filipek

Evening Short Prayer

Photo by Matej Rieciciar

Come Before God

Ask for God's Help to Pray

Psalm 36:7, 9

How excellent is your mercy, O God! The children of men shall take refuge under the shadow of your wings. For with you is the well of life, and in your light shall we see light.

Celebrate God's Beauty

Pray the Phos Hilaron

1979 Book of Common Prayer‡

O gladdening light, pure brightness of the everliving Father in heaven, O Jesus Christ, holy and blessed!

Now as we come to the setting of the sun, and our eyes behold the vesper light, we sing your praises, O God: Father, Son, and Holy Spirit.

You are worthy at all times to be praised by happy voices, O Son of God, O Giver of Life, and to be glorified through all the worlds.

Learn

Read the passage of the day or follow another reading plan. Devotional lessons from other sources than the Bible can also be read at this time. For other reading plans, see the Lectionary on page 64 and the Psalter on page 88.

Monday

Jesus spoke to them, saying, "I am the light of the world. Whoever follows me will not walk in darkness, but will have the light of life."

John 8:12

Sunday

For what we proclaim is not ourselves, but Jesus Christ as Lord, with ourselves as your servants for Jesus' sake. For God, who said, "Let light shine out of darkness," has shone in our hearts, to give the light of the knowledge of the glory of God in the face of Jesus Christ.

II Corinthians 4:5-6

Tuesday

Jesus said, "Behold, I stand at the door and knock. If anyone hears my voice and opens the door, I will come in to him and eat with him, and he with me."

Revelation 3:20

Wednesday

For I am sure that neither death nor life, nor angels nor rulers, nor things present nor things to come, nor powers, nor height nor depth, nor anything else in all creation, will be able to separate us from the love of God in Christ Jesus our Lord.

Romans 8:38-39

Thursday

You keep them in perfect peace whose minds are stayed on you, because they trust in you. Trust in the LORD for ever, for the LORD God is an everlasting rock.

Isaiah 26:3-4

Friday

Now may the God of peace himself sanctify you completely, and may your whole spirit and soul and body be kept blameless at the coming of our Lord Jesus Christ.

I Thessalonians 5:23

Saturday

Come, bless the LORD, all you servants of the LORD, who stand by night in the house of the LORD! Lift up your hands to the holy place and bless the LORD! May the LORD bless you from Zion, he who made heaven and earth!

Psalm 134

Keep Silence

Quiet Your Soul before God

Keep silence for one minute.

Consider this a time of wordless prayer. If your mind is full of distraction, pray one of these simple prayers repeatedly.

- Jesus.
- Jesus Christ, Son of God, have mercy on me, a sinner.
- Jesus, I am safe with you.
- Jesus is enough.
- Lord, I am here with you, and you are here with me.
- Behold the Lamb of God, who takes away the sin of the world.

It may be helpful to predetermine the amount of time to be spent in silence and use a timer.

Offer Petitions, Intercessions, and Thanks

Feel free to simply bring needs before God and follow this format:

For _____:
Lord, have mercy. Christ, have mercy.

Offer Gratitude for 3 Things

Keep a List of Repeated Prayers

Family, friends, enemies, the suffering, desires, fears, needs, the culture, the world

If you are following the morning office and/or other times of prayer as well, divide your list among prayer times however seems wise and fits your schedule.

Pray for Those Who Come to Mind

Affirm the Faith

Recite the Nicene Creed

1979 Book of Common Prayer

STAND.

We believe in one God, the Father, the Almighty, maker of heaven and earth, of all that is, seen and unseen.

We believe in one Lord, Jesus Christ, the only Son of God, eternally begotten of the Father, God from God, Light from Light, true God from true God, begotten, not made, of one Being with the Father. Through him all things were made. For us and for our salvation he came down from heaven: by the power of the Holy Spirit he became incarnate from the Virgin Mary, and was made man. For our sake he was crucified under Pontius Pilate; he suffered death and was buried.

On the third day he rose again in accordance with the Scriptures; he ascended into heaven and is seated at the right hand of the Father. He will come again in glory to judge the living and the dead, and his kingdom will have no end.

We believe in the Holy Spirit, the Lord, the giver of life, who proceeds from the Father and the Son. With the Father and the Son he is worshiped and glorified. He has spoken through the Prophets. We believe in one holy catholic and apostolic Church. We acknowledge one baptism for the forgiveness of sins. We look for the resurrection of the dead, and the life of the world to come.

Amen.

Pray as Jesus Taught

Pray the Lord's Prayer

1979 Book of Common Prayer; Mt. 6:9–13

Kneel.

Our Father, who art in heaven, hallowed be Thy name.

Thy Kingdom come, Thy will be done, on earth as it is in heaven.

Give us this day our daily bread;

And forgive us our trespasses as we forgive those who trespass against us.

And lead us not into temptation, but deliver us from evil.

For Thine is the Kingdom, the power, and the glory for ever and ever. Amen.

Rise.

Pray the Collect

A Collect for Christ's Presence

1979 Book of Common Prayer

Lord Jesus, stay with us, for evening is at hand and the day is past; be our companion in the way, kindle our hearts, and awaken hope, that we may know you as you are revealed in Scripture and the breaking of bread. Grant this for the sake of your love. Amen.

✝

Guide us waking, O Lord, and guard us sleeping; that awake we may watch with Christ, and asleep we may rest in peace.

Amen.

Photo by Sergio Rodriguez - Portugues del Olmo

Appendices

Lectionary

January: Morning or Odd Years

DATE (FEAST DAY)	PSALMS	FIRST LESSON	SECOND LESSON
1 (Circumcision & Name)	1, 2	Gen 1	John 1:1-28
2	5, 6	Gen 2	John 1:29-end
3	9	Gen 3	John 2
4	8, 11	Gen 4	John 3:1-21
5	12, 13, 14	Gen 5	John 3:22-end
6 (Epiphany)	96, 97	Gen 6	Matt 2:1-12
7	18:1-19	Gen 7	John 4:1-26
8	19	Gen 8	John 4:27-end
9	22	Gen 9	John 5:1-24
10	25	Gen 10 † 1-9,15-22,30-32	John 5:25-end
11	26, 28	Gen 11 † 1-9,27-32	John 6:1-21
12	29, 30	Gen 12	John 6:22-40
13	34	Gen 13	John 6:41-end
14	32, 36	Gen 14	John 7:1-24
15	37:1-22	Gen 15	John 7:25-52
16	40	Gen 16	John 7:53—8:30
17	42, 43	Gen 17	John 8:31-end
18 (Peter's Confession)	45	Gen 18	Matt 16:13-20
19	47, 48	Gen 19 † 1-29	John 9
20	50	Gen 20	John 10:1-21
21	52, 53, 54	Gen 21 † 1-21	John 10:22-end
22	56, 57	Gen 22	John 11:1-44
23	59	Gen 23	John 11:45-end
24	61, 62	Gen 24 † 1-28,53-58	John 12:1-19
25 (Paul's Conversion)	68:1-18	Acts 9:1-22	John 12:20-end
26	69:1-19	Gen 25 † 7-11,19-34	John 13
27	66	Gen 26 † 1-25	John 14:1-14
28	71	Gen 27 † 1-13,18-36,39-40	John 14:15-end
29	74	Gen 28	John 15:1-17
30	75, 76	Gen 29 † 1-28	John 15:18-end
31	78:1-16	Gen 30 † 1-2,22-43	John 16:1-15

† Indicates a portion which may be read optionally instead of the whole chapter

Feast days (noted in parentheses) have their own particular collects (see page 90) that may be prayed instead of the daily collects that follow the Lessons.

JANUARY: EVENING OR EVEN YEARS

DATE (FEAST DAY)	PSALMS	FIRST LESSON	SECOND LESSON
1 (Circumcision & Name)	3, 4	Gal 1	Luke 2:8-21
2	7	Jer 1	Gal 2
3	10	Jer 2 † 1-22	Gal 3
4	15, 16	Jer 3	Gal 4
5	17	Jer 4	Gal 5
6 (Epiphany)	67, 72	Jer 5	John 2:1-12
7	18:20-50	Jer 6	Gal 6
8	20, 21	Jer 7 † 1-28,34	1 Thess 1
9	23, 24	Jer 8	1 Thess 2:1-16
10	27	Jer 9	1 Thess 2:17—3 end
11	31	Jer 10	1 Thess 4:1-12
12	33	Jer 11	1 Thess 4:13—5:11
13	35	Jer 12	1 Thess 5:12-end
14	38	Jer 13	2 Thess 1
15	37:23-40	Jer 14	2 Thess 2
16	39, 41	Jer 15	2 Thess 3
17	44	Jer 16	1 Cor 1:1-25
18 (Peter's Confession)	46	Jer 17	1 Cor 1:26—2 end
19	49	Jer 18	1 Cor 3
20	51	Jer 19	1 Cor 4:1-17
21	55	Jer 20	1 Cor 4:18—5 end
22	58, 60	Jer 21	1 Cor 6
23	63, 64	Jer 22	1 Cor 7
24	65, 67	Jer 23 † 1-9,16-18,21-40	1 Cor 8
25 (Paul's Conversion)	68:19-35	Jer 24	1 Cor 9
26	69:20-36	Jer 25 † 1-19,26-31	1 Cor 10
27	70, 72	Jer 26	1 Cor 11
28	73	Jer 27	1 Cor 12
29	77	Jer 28	1 Cor 13
30	79, 82	Jer 29 † 1-14,24-32	1 Cor 14:1-19
31	78:17-39	Jer 30	1 Cor 14:20-end

† *Indicates a portion which may be read optionally instead of the whole chapter*

Feast days (noted in parentheses) have their own particular collects (see page 90) that may be prayed instead of the daily collects that follow the Lessons.

Ash Wednesday and the following holy days that include and depend on the date of Easter have particular lessons. See page 89 for the list of days and the lessons.

FEBRUARY: MORNING OR ODD YEARS

DATE (FEAST DAY)	PSALMS	FIRST LESSON	SECOND LESSON
1	78:40-72	Gen 31 † 1-3,17-45	John 16:16-end
2 (Presentation)	24, 81	Gen 32 † 1-13,21-32	Luke 2:22-40
3	83	Gen 33	John 17
4	86, 87	Gen 34	John 18:1-27
5	89:1-18	Gen 35	John 18:28-end
6	90	Gen 36 † 1-8	John 19:1-37
7	92, 93	Gen 37 † 3-8,12-36	John 19:38-end
8	95, 96	Gen 38 † 1-26	John 20
9	99, 100, 101	Gen 39	John 21
10	103	Gen 40	Matt 1:1-17
11	105:1-24	Gen 41 † 1-15,25-40	Matt 1:18-end
12	106:1-18	Gen 42 † 1-28	Matt 2
13	107:1-22	Gen 43 † 1-10,15-34	Matt 3
14	108, 110	Gen 44 † 1-20,30-34	Matt 4
15	111, 112	Gen 45	Matt 5:1-20
16	115	Gen 46 † 1-7,28-34	Matt 5:21-48
17	119:1-24	Gen 47 † 1-15,23-31	Matt 6:1-18
18	119:49-72	Gen 48	Matt 6:19-end
19	119:89-104	Gen 49	Matt 7
20	119:129-152	Gen 50	Matt 8:1-17
21	118	Exod 1	Matt 8:18-end
22	122, 123	Exod 2	Matt 9:1-17
23	127, 128	Exod 3	Matt 9:18-34
24 (Matthias)	132, 133	Acts 1:15-26	Matt 9:35—10:23
25	136	Exod 4	Matt 10:24-end
26	139	Exod 5	Matt 11
27	140	Exod 6 † 1-13	Matt 12:1-21
28	144	Exod 7	Matt 12:22-end
29	90	2 Kings 2	Luke 24:44-53

Feast days (noted in parentheses) have their own particular collects (see page 90) that may be prayed instead of the daily collects that follow the Lessons.

Ash Wednesday and the following holy days that include and depend on the date of Easter have particular lessons. See page 89 for the list of days and the lessons.

FEBRUARY: EVENING OR EVEN YEARS

DATE (FEAST DAY)	PSALMS	FIRST LESSON	SECOND LESSON
1	80	Jer 31 † 1-17,27-37	1 Cor 15:1-34
2 (Presentation)	84	Jer 32 † 1-15,36-44	1 Cor 15:35-end
3	85	Jer 33	1 Cor 16
4	88	Jer 34	2 Cor 1:1—2:11
5	89:19-52	Jer 35	2 Cor 2:12—3 end
6	91	Jer 36 † 1-10,19-32	2 Cor 4
7	94	Jer 37	2 Cor 5
8	97, 98	Jer 38	2 Cor 6
9	102	Jer 39	2 Cor 7
10	104	Jer 40	2 Cor 8
11	105:25-45	Jer 41	2 Cor 9
12	106:19-48	Jer 42	2 Cor 10
13	107:23-43	Jer 43	2 Cor 11
14	109	Jer 44 † 1-19,24-30	2 Cor 12:1-13
15	113, 114	Jer 45	2 Cor 12:14—13 end
16	116, 117	Jer 46	Rom 1
17	119:25-48	Jer 47	Rom 2
18	119:73-88	Jer 48 † 1-20,40-47	Rom 3
19	119:105-128	Jer 49 † 1-13,23-39	Rom 4
20	119:153-176	Jer 50 † 1-20,33-40	Rom 5
21	120, 121	Jer 51 † 6-10,45-64	Rom 6
22	124, 125, 126	Jer 52 † 1-27,31-34	Rom 7
23	129, 130, 131	—	Rom 8:1-17
24 (Matthias)	134, 135	—	Rom 8:18-end
25	137, 138	Lam 1 † 1-12,17-22	Rom 9
26	141, 142	Lam 2 † 1-18	Rom 10
27	143	Lam 3 † 1-9,19-33,52-66	Rom 11
28	145	Lam 4	Rom 12
29	104	Joel 2 † 1-2,12-32	2 Peter 3

Feast days (noted in parentheses) have their own particular collects (see page 90) that may be prayed instead of the daily collects that follow the Lessons.

Ash Wednesday and the following holy days that include and depend on the date of Easter have particular lessons. See page 89 for the list of days and the lessons.

March: Morning or Odd Years

DATE (FEAST DAY)	PSALMS	FIRST LESSON	SECOND LESSON
1	146	Exod 8	Matt 13:1-23
2	148	Exod 9 † 1-29,33-34	Matt 13:24-43
3	1, 2	Exod 10	Matt 13:44-end
4	5, 6	Exod 11	Matt 14
5	9	Exod 12 † 1-20,28-36	Matt 15:1-28
6	8, 11	Exod 13	Matt 15:29—16:12
7	12, 13, 14	Exod 14 † 5-31	Matt 16:13-end
8	18:1-19	Exod 15	Matt 17:1-23
9	19	Exod 16 † 1-7,11-33	Matt 17:24—18:14
10	22	Exod 17	Matt 18:15-end
11	25	Exod 18	Matt 19:1-15
12	26, 28	Exod 19	Matt 19:16—20:16
13	29, 30	Exod 20	Matt 20:17-end
14	34	Exod 21 † 1-19,22-29	Matt 21:1-22
15	32, 36	Exod 22	Matt 21:23-end
16	37:1-22	Exod 23 † 1-13,18-30	Matt 22:1-33
17	40	Exod 24	Matt 22:34—23:12
18	42, 43	Exod 25 † 1-23,31-40	Matt 23:13-end
19 (Joseph)	45	Exod 26 † 1-10,15-16,29-37	Matt 24:1-28
20	47, 48	Exod 27	Matt 24:29-end
21	50	Exod 28 † 1-6,15-21, 29-43	Matt 25:1-30
22	52, 53, 54	Exod 29 † 1-18,35-46	Matt 25:31-end
23	56, 57	Exod 30 † 1-3,7-33	Matt 26:1-30
24	59	Exod 31	Matt 26:31-56
25 (Annunciation)	113, 138	Exod 32 † 1-29	Luke 1:26-38
26	61, 62	Exod 33	Matt 26:57-end
27	68:1-18	Exod 34 † 1-17,27-35	Matt 27:1-26
28	69:1-19	Exod 35 † 1-10,20-35	Matt 27:27-56
29	66	Exod 36 † 1-10,18-20, 31-38	Matt 27:57—28 end
30	71	Exod 37 † 1-11,16-29	Mark 1:1-13
31	74	Exod 38 † 1-23	Mark 1:14-31

† Indicates a portion which may be read optionally instead of the whole chapter

Feast days (noted in parentheses) have their own particular collects (see page 90) that may be prayed instead of the daily collects that follow the Lessons.

Ash Wednesday and the following holy days that include and depend on the date of Easter have particular lessons. See page 89 for the list of days and the lessons.

MARCH: EVENING OR EVEN YEARS

DATE (FEAST DAY)	PSALMS	FIRST LESSON	SECOND LESSON
1	147	Lam 5	Rom 13
2	149, 150	Prov 1	Rom 14
3	3, 4	Prov 2	Rom 15
4	7	Prov 3 † 1-27	Rom 16
5	10	Prov 4	Phil 1:1-11
6	15, 16	Prov 5	Phil 1:12-end
7	17	Prov 6 † 1-11, 20-35	Phil 2:1-11
8	18:20-50	Prov 7	Phil 2:12-end
9	20, 21	Prov 8	Phil 3
10	23, 24	Prov 9	Phil 4
11	27	Prov 10	Col 1:1-20
12	31	Prov 11	Col 1:21—2:7
13	33	Prov 12	Col 2:8-19
14	35	Prov 13	Col 2:20—3:11
15	38	Prov 14	Col 3:12-end
16	37:23-40	Prov 15	Col 4
17	39, 41	Prov 16	Philemon
18	44	Prov 17	Eph 1:1-14
19 (Joseph)	46	Eph 1:15-end	Matt 1:18-end
20	49	Prov 18	Eph 2:1-10
21	51	Prov 19	Eph 2:11-end
22	55	Prov 20	Eph 3
23	58, 60	Prov 21	Eph 4:1-16
24	63, 64	Prov 22	Eph 4:17-end
25 (Annunciation)	131, 132	Prov 23	Eph 5:1-17
26	65, 67	Prov 24 † 1-14, 23-34	Eph 5:18-end
27	68:19-35	Prov 25	Eph 6:1-9
28	69:20-36	Prov 26	Eph 6:10-end
29	70, 72	Prov 27	1 Tim 1:1-17
30	73	Prov 28	1 Tim 1:18—2 end
31	77	Prov 29	1 Tim 3

† Indicates a portion which may be read optionally instead of the whole chapter

Feast days (noted in parentheses) have their own particular collects (see page 90) that may be prayed instead of the daily collects that follow the Lessons.

Ash Wednesday and the following holy days that include and depend on the date of Easter have particular lessons. See page 89 for the list of days and the lessons.

APRIL: MORNING OR ODD YEARS

DATE (FEAST DAY)	PSALMS	FIRST LESSON	SECOND LESSON
1	75, 76	Exod 39 † 1-14,27-43	Mark 1:32-end
2	78:1-16	Exod 40 † 1-2,16-38	Mark 2:1-22
3	78:40-72	Lev 1	Mark 2:23—3:12
4	81	Lev 8 † 1-24,30-36	Mark 3:13-end
5	84	Lev 10	Mark 4:1-34
6	86, 87	Lev 16 † 1-22,29-34	Mark 4:35—5:20
7	89:1-18	Lev 17	Mark 5:21-end
8	90	Lev 18	Mark 6:1-29
9	92, 93	Lev 19 † 1-2,9-37	Mark 6:30-end
10	95, 96	Lev 20	Mark 7:1-23
11	99, 100, 101	Lev 23 † 9-32,39-43	Mark 7:24—8:10
12	103	Lev 26 † 3-20,38-46	Mark 8:11-end
13	105:1-24	Num 6	Mark 9:1-29
14	106:1-18	Num 8 † 5-26	Mark 9:30-end
15	107:1-22	Num 11 † 4-6,10-33	Mark 10:1-31
16	108, 110	Num 12	Mark 10:32-end
17	111, 112	Num 13 † 1-3,17-33	Mark 11:1-26
18	115	Num 14 † 1-31	Mark 11:27—12:12
19	119:1-24	Num 15 † 22-41	Mark 12:13-34
20	119:49-72	Num 16 † 1-11,20-38	Mark 12:35—13:13
21	119:89-104	Num 17	Mark 13:14-end
22	119:129-152	Num 18 † 1-24	Mark 14:1-25
23	118	Num 20	Mark 14:26-52
24	122, 123	Num 21 † 4-9,21-35	Mark 14:53-end
25 (Mark)	127, 128	Acts 12:11-25	Mark 15
26	132, 133	Num 22 † 1-35	Mark 16
27	136	Num 23 † 1-26	Luke 1:1-23
28	139	Num 24	Luke 1:24-56
29	140	Num 25	Luke 1:57-end
30	144	Deut 1 † 1-21,26-33	Luke 2:1-21

Feast days (noted in parentheses) have their own particular collects (see page 90) that may be prayed instead of the daily collects that follow the Lessons.

Ash Wednesday and the following holy days that include and depend on the date of Easter have particular lessons. See page 89 for the list of days and the lessons.

APRIL: EVENING OR EVEN YEARS

DATE (FEAST DAY)	PSALMS	FIRST LESSON	SECOND LESSON
1	79, 82	Prov 30 † 1-9,15-33	1 Tim 4
2	78:17-39	Prov 31	1 Tim 5
3	80	Job 1	1 Tim 6
4	83	Job 2	Titus 1
5	85	Job 3	Titus 2
6	88	Job 4	Titus 3
7	89:19-52	Job 5	2 Tim 1
8	91	Job 6	2 Tim 2
9	94	Job 7	2 Tim 3
10	97, 98	Job 8	2 Tim 4
11	102	Job 9	Heb 1
12	104	Job 10	Heb 2
13	105:23-44	Job 11	Heb 3
14	106:19-48	Job 12	Heb 4:1-13
15	107:23-43	Job 13	Heb 4:14—5:10
16	109	Job 14	Heb 5:11—6 end
17	113, 114	Job 15	Heb 7
18	116, 117	Job 16	Heb 8
19	119:25-48	Job 17	Heb 9:1-14
20	119:73-88	Job 18	Heb 9:15-end
21	119:105-128	Job 19	Heb 10:1-18
22	119:153-176	Job 20	Heb 10:19-end
23	120, 121	Job 21	Heb 11
24	124, 125, 126	Job 22	Heb 12:1-17
25 (Mark)	129, 130, 131	Job 23	Heb 12:18-end
26	134, 135	Job 24	Heb 13
27	137, 138	Job 25 & 26	Jas 1
28	141, 142	Job 27	Jas 2:1-13
29	143	Job 28	Jas 2:14-end
30	145	Job 29	Jas 3

Feast days (noted in parentheses) have their own particular collects (see page 90) that may be prayed instead of the daily collects that follow the Lessons.

Ash Wednesday and the following holy days that include and depend on the date of Easter have particular lessons. See page 89 for the list of days and the lessons.

MAY: MORNING OR ODD YEARS

DATE (FEAST DAY)	PSALMS	FIRST LESSON	SECOND LESSON
1 (Philip & James the Less)	146	Deut 2 † 1-9,14-19,24-37	Luke 2:22-end
2	148	Deut 3	Luke 3:1-22
3	1, 2	Deut 4 † 1-18,24-40	Luke 3:23-end
4	5, 6	Deut 5	Luke 4:1-30
5	9	Deut 6	Luke 4:31-end
6	8, 11	Deut 7	Luke 5:1-16
7	12, 13, 14	Deut 8	Luke 5:17-end
8	18:1-19	Deut 9	Luke 6:1-19
9	19	Deut 10	Luke 6:20-38
10	22	Deut 11	Luke 6:39—7:10
11	25	Deut 12	Luke 7:11-35
12	26, 28	Deut 13	Luke 7:36-end
13	29, 30	Deut 14	Luke 8:1-21
14	34	Deut 15	Luke 8:22-end
15	32, 36	Deut 16	Luke 9:1-17
16	37:1-22	Deut 17	Luke 9:18-50
17	40	Deut 18	Luke 9:51-end
18	42, 43	Deut 19	Luke 10:1-24
19	45	Deut 20	Luke 10:25-end
20	47, 48	Deut 21	Luke 11:1-28
21	50	Deut 22	Luke 11:29-end
22	52, 53, 54	Deut 23	Luke 12:1-34
23	56, 57	Deut 24	Luke 12:35-53
24	59	Deut 25	Luke 12:54—13:9
25	61, 62	Deut 26	Luke 13:10-end
26	68:1-18	Deut 27	Luke 14:1-24
27	69:1-19	Deut 28 † 1-25,64-68	Luke 14:25—15:10
28	66	Deut 29	Luke 15:11-end
29	71	Deut 30	Luke 16
30	74	Deut 31	Luke 17:1-19
31 (Visitation)	75, 76	Deut 32 † 1-10,15-22,39-52	Luke 1:39-56

† *Indicates a portion which may be read optionally instead of the whole chapter*

Feast days (noted in parentheses) have their own particular collects (see page 90) that may be prayed instead of the daily collects that follow the Lessons.

Ash Wednesday and the following holy days that include and depend on the date of Easter have particular lessons. See page 89 for the list of days and the lessons.

MAY: EVENING OR EVEN YEARS

DATE (FEAST DAY)	PSALMS	FIRST LESSON	SECOND LESSON
1 (Philip & James the Less)	147	Jas 4	John 1:43-end
2	149, 150	Job 30	Jas 5
3	3, 4	Job 31 † 1-23,35-40	1 Pet 1:1-21
4	7	Job 32	1 Pet 1:22—2:10
5	10	Job 33	1 Pet 2:11—3:7
6	15, 16	Job 34 † 1-15,21-28,31-37	1 Pet 3:8—4:6
7	17	Job 35	1 Pet 4:7-end
8	18:20-50v	Job 36	1 Pet 5
9	20, 21	Job 37	2 Pet 1
10	23, 24	Job 38 † 1-27,31-33	2 Pet 2
11	27	Job 39	2 Pet 3
12	31	Job 40	Jude
13	33	Job 41	1 John 1:1—2:6
14	35	Job 42	1 John 2:7-end
15	38	Eccl 1	1 John 3:1-10
16	37:23-40v	Eccl 2	1 John 3:11—4:6
17	39, 41	Eccl 3	1 John 4:7-end
18	44	Eccl 4	1 John 5
19	46	Eccl 5	2 John
20	49	Eccl 6	3 John
21	51	Eccl 7	Acts 1:1-14
22	55	Eccl 8	Acts 1:15-end
23	58, 60	Eccl 9	Acts 2:1-21
24	63, 64	Eccl 10	Acts 2:22-end
25	65, 67	Eccl 11	Acts 3:1—4:4
26	68:19-35 v	Eccl 12	Acts 4:5-31
27	69:20-36v	Ezek 1	Acts 4:32—5:11
28	70, 72	Ezek 2	Acts 5:12-end
29	73	Ezek 3	Acts 6:1—7:16
30	77	Ezek 4	Acts 7:17-34
31 (Visitation)	79, 82	Ezek 5	Acts 7:35—8:3

† *Indicates a portion which may be read optionally instead of the whole chapter*

Feast days (noted in parentheses) have their own particular collects (see page 90) that may be prayed instead of the daily collects that follow the Lessons.

Ash Wednesday and the following holy days that include and depend on the date of Easter have particular lessons. See page 89 for the list of days and the lessons.

JUNE: MORNING OR ODD YEARS

DATE (FEAST DAY)	PSALMS	FIRST LESSON	SECOND LESSON
1	78:1-16	Deut 33	Luke 17:20-end
2	78:40-72	Deut 34	Luke 18:1-30
3	81	Josh 1	Luke 18:31—19:10
4	84	Josh 2	Luke 19:11-28
5	86, 87	Josh 3	Luke 19:29-end
6	89:1-18	Josh 4	Luke 20:1-26
7	90	Josh 5	Luke 20:27—21:4
8	92, 93	Josh 6	Luke 21:5-end
9	95, 96	Josh 7	Luke 22:1-38
10	99, 100, 101	Josh 8 † 1-22,30-35	Luke 22:39-53
11 (Barnabas)	103	Acts 4:32-37	Luke 22:54-end
12	105:1-24	Josh 9	Luke 23:1-25
13	106:1-18	Josh 10 † 1-27,40-43	Luke:23:26-49
14	107:1-22	Josh 14 † 5-15	Luke 23:50—24:12
15	108, 110	Josh 22 † 7-31	Luke 24:13-end
16	111, 112	Josh 23	Gal 1
17	115	Josh 24 † 1-31	Gal 2
18	119:1-24	Judg 1 † 1-21	Gal 3
19	119:49-72	Judg 2 † 6-23	Gal 4
20	119:89-104	Judg 3 † 7-30	Gal 5
21	119:129-152	Judg 4	Gal 6
22	118	Judg 5 † 1-5,19-31	1 Thess 1
23	122, 123	Judg 6 † 1,6,11-24,33-40	1 Thess 2:1-16
24 (Nativity of John Bap.)	127, 128	1 Thess 2:17—3 end	Matt 14:1-13
25	132, 133	Judg 7 † 1-8,16-25	1 Thess 4:1-12
26	136	Judg 8 † 4-23,28	1 Thess 4:13—5:11
27	139	Judg 9 † 1-6,22-25,43-56	1 Thess 5:12-end
28	140	Judg 10 † 6-18	2 Thess 1
29 (Peter & Paul)	144	2 Thess 2	2 Pet 3:14-end
30	146	Judg 11 † 1-11,29-40	2 Thess 3

† *Indicates a portion which may be read optionally instead of the whole chapter*

Feast days (noted in parentheses) have their own particular collects (see page 90) that may be prayed instead of the daily collects that follow the Lessons.

Ash Wednesday and the following holy days that include and depend on the date of Easter have particular lessons. See page 89 for the list of days and the lessons.

JUNE: EVENING OR EVEN YEARS

DATE (FEAST DAY)	PSALMS	FIRST LESSON	SECOND LESSON
1	78:17-39v	Ezek 6	Acts 8:4-25
2	80	Ezek 7	Acts 8:26-end
3	83	Ezek 8	Acts 9:1-31
4	85	Ezek 9	Acts 9:32-end
5	88	Ezek 10	Acts 10:1-23
6	89:19-52	Ezek 11	Acts 10:24-end
7	91	Ezek 12	Acts 11:1-18
8	94	Ezek 13	Acts 11:19-end
9	97, 98	Ezek 14	Acts 12:1-24
10	102	Ezek 15	Acts 12:25—13:12
11 (Barnabas)	104	Ezek 16 † 1-15,33-47, 59-63	Acts 13:13-43
12	105:25-45	Ezek 17	Acts 13:44—14:7
13	106:19-48	Ezek 18	Acts 14:8-end
14	107:23-43	Ezek 33 † 1-23,30-33	Acts 15:1-21
15	109	Ezek 34	Acts 15:22-35
16	113, 114	Ezek 35	Acts 15:36—16:5
17	116, 117	Ezek 36 † 16-37 † 16-37	Acts 16:6-end
18	119:25-48	Ezek 37	Acts 17:1-15
19	119:73-88	Ezek 40 † 1-5,17-19,35-49	Acts 17:16-end
20	119:105-128	Ezek 43	Acts 18:1-23
21	119:153-176	Ezek 47	Acts 18:24—19:7
22	120, 121	Dan 1	Acts 19:8-20
23	124, 125, 126	Dan 2 † 1-14,25-28,31-45	Acts 19:21-end
24 (Nativity of John Bap.)	129, 130, 131	Dan 3	Acts 20:1-16
25	134, 135	Dan 4 † 1-9,19-35	Acts 20:17-end
26	137, 138	Dan 5	Acts 21:1-16
27	141, 142	Dan 6	Acts 21:17-36
28	143	Dan 7	Acts 21:37—22:22
29 (Peter & Paul)	145	Dan 8	Acts 22:23—23:11
30	147	Dan 9	Acts 23:12-end

† *Indicates a portion which may be read optionally instead of the whole chapter*

Feast days (noted in parentheses) have their own particular collects (see page 90) that may be prayed instead of the daily collects that follow the Lessons.

JULY: MORNING OR ODD YEARS

DATE (FEAST DAY)	PSALMS	FIRST LESSON	SECOND LESSON
1	148	Judg 12	1 Cor 1:1-25
2	1, 2	Judg 13	1 Cor 1:26—2 end
3	5, 6	Judg 14	1 Cor 3
4	9	Judg 15	1 Cor 4:1-17
5	8, 11	Judg 16	1 Cor 4:18—5 end
6	12, 13, 14	Ruth 1	1 Cor 6
7	18:1-19	Ruth 2	1 Cor 7
8	19	Ruth 3	1 Cor 8
9	22	Ruth 4	1 Cor 9
10	25	1 Sam 1 † 1-20	1 Cor 10
11	26, 28	1 Sam 2 † 1-21	1 Cor 11
12	29, 30	1 Sam 3	1 Cor 12
13	34	1 Sam 4	1 Cor 13
14	32, 36	1 Sam 5	1 Cor 14:1-19
15	37:1-22	1 Sam 6 † 1-15	1 Cor 14:20-end
16	40	1 Sam 7	1 Cor 15:1-34
17	42, 43	1 Sam 8	1 Cor 15:35-end
18	45	1 Sam 9	1 Cor 16
19	47, 48	1 Sam 10	2 Cor 1:1—2:11
20	50	1 Sam 11	2 Cor 2:12—3 end
21	52, 53, 54	1 Sam 12	2 Cor 4
22 (Mary Magdalene)	56, 57	2 Cor 5	Luke 7:36—8:3
23	59	1 Sam 13	2 Cor 6
24	61, 62	1 Sam 14 † 1-15,20,24-30	2 Cor 7
25 (James, Son of Zebedee)	68:1-18	2 Cor 8	Mark 1:14-20
26	69:1-19	1 Sam 15	2 Cor 9
27	66	1 Sam 16	2 Cor 10
28	71	1 Sam 17 † 1-11,26-27,31-51	2 Cor 11
29	74	1 Sam 18	2 Cor 12:1-13
30	75, 76	1 Sam 19	2 Cor 12:14—13 end
31	78:1-16	1 Sam 20 † 1-7,24-42	Rom 1

† *Indicates a portion which may be read optionally instead of the whole chapter*

Feast days (noted in parentheses) have their own particular collects (see page 90) that may be prayed instead of the daily collects that follow the Lessons.

JULY: EVENING OR EVEN YEARS

DATE (FEAST DAY)	PSALMS	FIRST LESSON	SECOND LESSON
1	149, 150	Dan 10	Acts 24:1-23
2	3, 4	Dan 11 † 1-19	Acts 24:24—25:12
3	7	Dan 12	Acts 25:13-end
4	10	—	Acts 26
5	15, 16	Esth 1	Acts 27
6	17	Esth 2	Acts 28:1-15
7	18:20-50v	Esth 3	Acts 28:16-end
8	20, 21	Esth 4	Philemon
9	23, 24	Esth 5	1 Tim 1:1-17
10	27	Esth 6	1 Tim 1:18—2 end
11	31	Esth 7	1 Tim 3
12	33	Esth 8	1 Tim 4
13	35	Esth 9 & 10	1 Tim 5
14	38	Ezra 1	1 Tim 6
15	37:23-40v	Ezra 3	Titus 1
16	39, 41	Ezra 4	Titus 2
17	44	Ezra 5	Titus 3
18	46	Ezra 6	2 Tim 1
19	49	Ezra 7	2 Tim 2
20	51	Ezra 8 † 21-36	2 Tim 3
21	55	Ezra 9	2 Tim 4
22 (Mary Magdalene)	58, 60	Ezra 10 † 1-16	John 1:1-28
23	63, 64	Neh 1	John 1:29-end
24	65, 67	Neh 2	John 2
25 (James, Son of Zebedee)	68:19-35 v	Neh 3 † 1-15	John 3:1-21
26	69:20-36v	Neh 4	John 3:22-end
27	70, 72	Neh 5	John 4:1-26
28	73	Neh 6	John 4:27-end
29	77	Neh 8	John 5:1-24
30	79, 82	Neh 9 † 1-15,26-38	John 5:25-end
31	78:17-39v	Neh 10 † 28-39	John 6:1-21

† Indicates a portion which may be read optionally instead of the whole chapter

Feast days (noted in parentheses) have their own particular collects (see page 90) that may be prayed instead of the daily collects that follow the Lessons.

AUGUST: MORNING OR ODD YEARS

DATE (FEAST DAY)	PSALMS	FIRST LESSON	SECOND LESSON
1	78:40-72	1 Sam 21	Rom 2
2	81	1 Sam 22	Rom 3
3	84	1 Sam 23	Rom 4
4	86, 87	1 Sam 24	Rom 5
5	89:1-18	1 Sam 25 † 1-19,23-25,32-42	Rom 6
6 (Transfiguration)	27	Rom 7	Mark 9:2-10
7	90	1 Sam 26	Rom 8:1-17
8	92, 93	1 Sam 27	Rom 8:18-end
9	95, 96	1 Sam 28	Rom 9
10	99, 100, 101	1 Sam 29	Rom 10
11	103	1 Sam 30 † 1-25	Rom 11
12	105:1-24	1 Sam 31	Rom 12
13	106:1-18	2 Sam 1	Rom 13
14	107:1-22	2 Sam 2 † 1-17,26-31	Rom 14
15 (Mary Mother of Jesus)	108, 110	2 Sam 3 † 6-11,17-39	Luke 1:26-38
16	111, 112	2 Sam 4	Rom 15
17	115	2 Sam 5	Rom 16
18	119:1-24	2 Sam 6	Phil 1:1-11
19	119:49-72	2 Sam 7	Phil 1:12-end
20	119:89-104	2 Sam 8	Phil 2:1-11
21	119:129-152	2 Sam 9	Phil 2:12-end
22	118	2 Sam 10	Phil 3
23	122, 123	2 Sam 11	Phil 4
24 (Bartholomew)	127, 128	Col 1:1-20	Luke 6:12-16
25	132, 133	2 Sam 12 † 1-25	Col 1:21—2:7
26	136	2 Sam 13 † 1-29,38-39	Col 2:8-19
27	139	2 Sam 14 † 1-21,28	Col 2:20—3:11
28	140	2 Sam 15 † 1-18,23-25,32-34	Col 3:12-end
29	144	2 Sam 16	Col 4
30	146	2 Sam 17 † 1-23	Philemon
31	148	2 Sam 18 † 1-15,19-33	Eph 1:1-14

† Indicates a portion which may be read optionally instead of the whole chapter

Feast days (noted in parentheses) have their own particular collects (see page 90) that may be prayed instead of the daily collects that follow the Lessons.

AUGUST: EVENING OR EVEN YEARS

DATE (FEAST DAY)	PSALMS	FIRST LESSON	SECOND LESSON
1	80	Neh 12 † 27-47	John 6:22-40
2	83	Neh 13 † 1-22,30-31	John 6:41-end
3	85	Hos 1	John 7:1-24
4	88	Hos 2	John 7:25-52
5	89:19-52	Hos 3	John 7:53—8:30
6 (Transfiguration)	80	Hos 4	John 8:31-end
7	91	Hos 5	John 9
8	94	Hos 6	John 10:1-21
9	97, 98	Hos 7	John 10:22-end
10	102	Hos 8	John 11:1-44
11	104	Hos 9	John 11:45-end
12	105:25-45	Hos 10	John 12:1-19
13	106:19-48	Hos 11	John 12:20-end
14	107:23-43	Hos 12	John 13
15 (Mary Mother of Jesus)	109	Hos 13	John 14:1-14
16	113, 114	Hos 14	John 14:15-end
17	116, 117	Joel 1	John 15:1-17
18	119:25-48	Joel 2 † 1-17,28-32	John 15:18-end
19	119:73-88	Joel 3	John 16:1-15
20	119:105-128	Amos 1	John 16:16-end
21	119:153-176	Amos 2	John 17
22	120, 121	Amos 3	John 18:1-27
23	124, 125, 126	Amos 4	John 18:28-end
24 (Bartholomew)	129, 130, 131	Amos 5	John 19:1-37
25	134, 135	Amos 6	John 19:38-end
26	137, 138	Amos 7	John 20
27	141, 142	Amos 8	John 21
28	143	Amos 9	Matt 1:1-17
29	145	Obadiah	Matt 1:18-end
30	147	Jonah 1	Matt 2
31	149, 150	Jonah 2	Matt 3

† *Indicates a portion which may be read optionally instead of the whole chapter*

Feast days (noted in parentheses) have their own particular collects (see page 90) that may be prayed instead of the daily collects that follow the Lessons.

SEPTEMBER: MORNING OR ODD YEARS

DATE (FEAST DAY)	PSALMS	FIRST LESSON	SECOND LESSON
1	1, 2	2 Sam 19 † 1-30	Eph 1:15-end
2	5, 6	2 Sam 20	Eph 2:1-10
3	9	2 Sam 21	Eph 2:11-end
4	8, 11	2 Sam 22 † 1-7,14-20,32-51	Eph 3
5	12, 13, 14	2 Sam 23 † 1-23	Eph 4:1-16
6	18:1-19	2 Sam 24	Eph 4:17-end
7	19	1 Chron 22	Eph 5:1-17
8	22	1 Kings 1 † 1-18,29-40	Eph 5:18-end
9	25	1 Chron 28	Eph 6
10	26, 28	1 Kings 2 † 1-25	Heb 1
11	29, 30	1 Kings 3	Heb 2
12	34	1 Kings 4 † 1-6,20-34	Heb 3
13	32, 36	1 Kings 5	Heb 4:1-13
14 (Holy Cross)	37:1-22	Heb 4:14—5:10	John 12:23-33
15	40	1 Kings 6 † 1-7,11-30,37-38	Heb 5:11—6 end
16	42, 43	1 Kings 7 † 1-14,40-44, 47-51	Heb 7
17	45	1 Kings 8 † 1-11,22-30,54-63	Heb 8
18	47, 48	1 Kings 9 † 1-9,15-28	Heb 9:1-14
19	50	1 Kings 10 †1-13,23-29	Heb 9:15-end
20	52, 53, 54	1 Kings 11 † 1-14,23-33,41-43	Heb 10:1-18
21 (Matthew)	56, 57	Heb 10:19-end	Matt 9:9-13
22	59	1 Kings 12 † 1-20,25-30	Heb 11
23	61, 62	1 Kings 13 † 1-25,33-34	Heb 12:1-17
24	68:1-18	1 Kings 14	Heb 12:18-end
25	69:1-19	2 Chron 12	Heb 13
26	66	2 Chron 13	James 1
27	71	2 Chron 14	James 2:1-13
28	74	2 Chron 15	James 2:14-end
29 (Michael)	75, 76	Rev 12:7-12	James 3
30	78:1-16	2 Chron 16	James 4

† *Indicates a portion which may be read optionally instead of the whole chapter*

Feast days (noted in parentheses) have their own particular collects (see page 90) that may be prayed instead of the daily collects that follow the Lessons.

SEPTEMBER: EVENING OR EVEN YEARS

DATE (FEAST DAY)	PSALMS	FIRST LESSON	SECOND LESSON
1	3, 4	Jonah 3	Matt 4
2	7	Jonah 4	Matt 5:1-20
3	10	Mic 1	Matt 5:21-48
4	15, 16	Mic 2	Matt 6:1-18
5	17	Mic 3	Matt 6:19-end
6	18:20-50v	Mic 4	Matt 7
7	20, 21	Mic 5	Matt 8:1-17
8	23, 24	Mic 6	Matt 8:18-end
9	27	Mic 7	Matt 9:1-17
10	31	Nahum 1	Matt 9:18-34
11	33	Nahum 2	Matt 9:35—10:23
12	35	Nahum 3	Matt 10:24-end
13	38	Hab 1	Matt 11
14 (Holy Cross)	37:23-40v	Hab 2	Matt 12:1-21
15	39, 41	Hab 3	Matt 12:22-end
16	44	Zeph 1	Matt 13:1-23
17	46	Zeph 2	Matt 13:24-43
18	49	Zeph 3	Matt 13:44-end
19	51	Hag 1	Matt 14
20	55	Hag 2	Matt 15:1-28
21 (Matthew)	58, 60	Zech 1	Matt 15:29—16:12
22	63, 64	Zech 2	Matt 16:13-end
23	65, 67	Zech 3	Matt 17:1-23
24	68:19-35 v	Zech 4	Matt 17:24—18:14
25	69:20-36v	Zech 5	Matt 18:15-end
26	70, 72	Zech 6	Matt 19:1-15
27	73	Zech 7	Matt 19:16—20:16
28	77	Zech 8	Matt 20:17-end
29 (Michael)	79, 82	Zech 9	Matt 21:1-22
30	78:17-39v	Zech 10	Matt 21:23-end

† Indicates a portion which may be read optionally instead of the whole chapter

Feast days (noted in parentheses) have their own particular collects (see page 90) that may be prayed instead of the daily collects that follow the Lessons.

OCTOBER: MORNING OR ODD YEARS

DATE (FEAST DAY)	PSALMS	FIRST LESSON	SECOND LESSON
1	78:40-72	1 Kings 15 † 1-30	James 5
2	81	1 Kings 16 † 1-4,8-19,23-34	1 Pet 1:1-21
3	84	1 Kings 17	1 Pet 1:22—2:10
4	86, 87	1 Kings 18 † 1-8,17-46	1 Pet 2:11—3:7
5	89:1-18	1 Kings 19	1 Pet 3:8—4:6
6	90	1 Kings 20 † 1,13,21-43	1 Pet 4:7-end
7	92, 93	1 Kings 21	1 Pet 5
8	95, 96	1 Kings 22 † 1-23,29-38	2 Pet 1
9	99, 100, 101	2 Chron 20	2 Pet 2
10	103	2 Kings 1	2 Pet 3
11	105:1-24	2 Kings 2	Jude
12	106:1-18	2 Kings 3	1 John 1:1—2:6
13	107:1-22	2 Kings 4 † 8-37	1 John 2:7-end
14	108, 110	2 Kings 5	1 John 3:1-10
15	111, 112	2 Kings 6 † 1-24	1 John 3:11—4:6
16	115	2 Kings 7	1 John 4:7-end
17	119:1-24	2 Kings 8 † 1-19,25-27	1 John 5
18 (Luke)	119:49-72	2 John	Luke 1:1-4
19	119:89-104	2 Kings 9 † 1-26,30-37	3 John
20	119:129-152	2 Kings 10 † 1-11,18-31	Acts 1:1-14
21	118	2 Kings 11	Acts 1:15-end
22	122, 123	2 Kings 12	Acts 2:1-21
23 (James of Jerusalem)	127, 128	Acts 2:22-end	James 1
24	132, 133	2 Kings 13	Acts 3:1—4:4
25	136	2 Kings 14	Acts 4:5-31
26	139	2 Chron 26	Acts 4:32—5:11
27	140	2 Kings 15 † 1-29	Acts 5:12-end
28 (Simon & Jude)	144	Acts 6:1—7:16	John 14:15-31
29	146	2 Kings 16	Acts 7:17-34
30	148	2 Kings 17 † 1-28,41	Acts 7:35—8:3
31	2	2 Chron 28	Acts 8:4-25

† *Indicates a portion which may be read optionally instead of the whole chapter*

Feast days (noted in parentheses) have their own particular collects (see page 90) that may be prayed instead of the daily collects that follow the Lessons.

OCTOBER: EVENING OR EVEN YEARS

DATE (FEAST DAY)	PSALMS	FIRST LESSON	SECOND LESSON
1	80	Zech 11	Matt 22:1-33
2	83	Zech 12	Matt 22:34—23:12
3	85	Zech 13	Matt 23:13-end
4	88	Zech 14	Matt 24:1-28
5	89:19-52	Mal 1	Matt 24:29-end
6	91	Mal 2	Matt 25:1-30
7	94	Mal 3	Matt 25:31-end
8	97, 98	Mal 4	Matt 26:1-30
9	102	—	Matt 26:31-56
10	104	—	Matt 26:57-end
11	105:25-45	—	Matt 27:1-26
12	106:19-48	—	Matt 27:27-56
13	107:23-43	—	Matt 27:57—28 end
14	109	—	Mark 1:1-13
15	113, 114	—	Mark 1:14-31
16	116, 117	—	Mark 1:32-end
17	119:25-48	—	Mark 2:1-22
18 (Luke)	119:73-88	—	Mark 2:23—3:12
19	119:105-128	Isa 1	Mark 3:13-end
20	119:153-176	Isa 2	Mark 4:1-34
21	120, 121	Isa 3	Mark 4:35—5:20
22	124, 125, 126	Isa 4	Mark 5:21-end
23 (James of Jerusalem)	129, 130, 131	Isa 5	Mark 6:1-29
24	134, 135	Isa 6	Mark 6:30-end
25	137, 138	Isa 7	Mark 7:1-23
26	141, 142	Isa 8	Mark 7:24—8:10
27	143	Isa 9	Mark 8:11-end
28 (Simon & Jude)	145	Isa 10	Mark 9:1-29
29	147	Isa 11	Mark 9:30-end
30	149, 150	Isa 12	Mark 10:1-31
31	3, 4	Isa 13	Mark 10:32-end

† *Indicates a portion which may be read optionally instead of the whole chapter*

Feast days (noted in parentheses) have their own particular collects (see page 90) that may be prayed instead of the daily collects that follow the Lessons.

NOVEMBER: MORNING OR ODD YEARS

DATE (FEAST DAY)	PSALMS	FIRST LESSON	SECOND LESSON
1 (All Saints')	1, 15	Heb 11:32—12:2	Acts 8:26-end
2	5, 6	2 Chron 29 † 1-11,20-30,35-36	Acts 9:1-31
3	9	2 Chron 30 † 1-22,26-27	Acts 9:32-end
4	8, 11	2 Kings 18 † 1-13,17-30,35-37	Acts 10:1-23
5	12, 13, 14	2 Kings 19 † 1-20,29-31,35-37	Acts 10:24-end
6	18:1-19	2 Kings 20	Acts 11:1-18
7	19	2 Chron 33	Acts 11:19-end
8	22	2 Kings 21	Acts 12:1-24
9	25	2 Kings 22	Acts 12:25—13:12
10	26, 28	2 Kings 23 † 1-20,26-30	Acts 13:13-43
11	29, 30	2 Kings 24	Acts 13:44—14:7
12	34	2 Kings 25 † 1-22,25-30	Acts 14:8-end
13	32, 36	Prov 1	Acts 15:1-21
14	37:1-22	Prov 2	Acts 15:22-35
15	40	Prov 3	Acts 15:36—16:5
16	42, 43	Prov 4	Acts 16:6-end
17	45	Prov 5	Acts 17:1-15
18	47, 48	Prov 6	Acts 17:16-end
19	50	Prov 7	Acts 18:1-23
20	52, 53, 54	Prov 8	Acts 18:24—19:7
21	56, 57	Prov 9	Acts 19:8-20
22	59	Prov 10	Acts 19:21-end
23	61, 62	Prov 11	Acts 20:1-16
24	68:1-18	Prov 12	Acts 20:17-end
25	69:1-19	Prov 13	Acts 21:1-16
26	66	Prov 14	Acts 21:17-36
27	71	Prov 15	Acts 21:37—22:22
28	74	Prov 16	Acts 22:23—23:11
29	75, 76	Prov 17	Acts 23:12-end
30 (Andrew)	78:1-16	Prov 18	John 1:35-42

† *Indicates a portion which may be read optionally instead of the whole chapter*

Feast days (noted in parentheses) have their own particular collects (see page 90) that may be prayed instead of the daily collects that follow the Lessons.

NOVEMBER: EVENING OR EVEN YEARS

DATE (FEAST DAY)	PSALMS	FIRST LESSON	SECOND LESSON
1 (All Saints')	34	Isa 14	Rev 19:1-16
2	7	Isa 15	Mark 11:1-26
3	10	Isa 16	Mark 11:27—12:12
4	15, 16	Isa 17	Mark 12:13-34
5	17	Isa 18	Mark 12:35—13:13
6	18:20-50v	Isa 19	Mark 13:14-end
7	20, 21	Isa 20	Mark 14:1-25
8	23, 24	Isa 21	Mark 14:26-52
9	27	Isa 22	Mark 14:53-end
10	31	Isa 23	Mark 15
11	33	Isa 24	Mark 16
12	35	Isa 25	Luke 1:1-23
13	38	Isa 26	Luke 1:24-56
14	37:23-40v	Isa 27	Luke 1:57-end
15	39, 41	Isa 28	Luke 2:1-21
16	44	Isa 29	Luke 2:22-end
17	46	Isa 30	Luke 3:1-22
18	49	Isa 31	Luke 3:23-end
19	51	Isa 32	Luke 4:1-30
20	55	Isa 33	Luke 4:31-end
21	58, 60	Isa 34	Luke 5:1-16
22	63, 64	Isa 35	Luke 5:17-end
23	65, 67	Isa 36	Luke 6:1-19
24	68:19-35 v	Isa 37	Luke 6:20-38
25	69:20-36v	Isa 38	Luke 6:39—7:10
26	70, 72	Isa 39	Luke 7:11-35
27	73	Isa 40	Luke 7:36-end
28	77	Isa 41	Luke 8:1-21
29	79, 82	Isa 42	Luke 8:22-end
30 (Andrew)	78:17-39v	Isa 43	Luke 9:1-17

† *Indicates a portion which may be read optionally instead of the whole chapter*

Feast days (noted in parentheses) have their own particular collects (see page 90) that may be prayed instead of the daily collects that follow the Lessons.

DECEMBER: MORNING OR ODD YEARS

DATE (FEAST DAY)	PSALMS	FIRST LESSON	SECOND LESSON
1	78:40-72	Prov 19	Acts 24:1-23
2	81	Prov 20	Acts 24:24—25:12
3	84	Prov 21	Acts 25:13-end
4	86, 87	Prov 22	Acts 26
5	89:1-18	Prov 23	Acts 27
6	90	Prov 24	Acts 28:1-15
7	92, 93	Prov 25	Acts 28:16-end
8	95, 96	Prov 26	Rev 1
9	99, 100, 101	Prov 27	Rev 2:1-17
10	103	Prov 28	Rev 2:18—3:6
11	105:1-24	Prov 29	Rev 3:7-end
12	106:1-18	Prov 30	Rev 4
13	107:1-22	Prov 31	Rev 5
14	108, 110	Lam 1	Rev 6
15	111, 112	Lam 2	Rev 7
16	115	Lam 3	Rev 8
17	119:1-24	Lam 4	Rev 9
18	119:49-72	Lam 5	Rev 10
19	119:89-104	Phil 1:1-11	Rev 11
20	119:129-152	Phil 1:12-end	Rev 12
21 (Thomas)	118	Rev 13	John 14:1-7
22	122, 123	Phil 2:1-11	Rev 14
23	127, 128	Phil 2:12-end	Rev 15
24 (Christmas Eve)	132, 133	Phil 3	Rev 16
25 (Christmas)	19 or 45	Isa 9:1-7	Rev 17
26 (Stephen)	136	Acts 6:8—7:6,17-41,44-60	Rev 18
27 (John)	139	Rev 19	John 21:9-25
28 (Innocents)	140	Jer 31:1-17	Rev 20
29	144	Phil 4	Rev 21:1-14
30	146	Ecc 3:1-13	Rev 21:15—22:5
31	148	Ecc 3:14-22	Rev 22:6-end

† *Indicates a portion which may be read optionally instead of the whole chapter*

Feast days (noted in parentheses) have their own particular collects (see page 90) that may be prayed instead of the daily collects that follow the Lessons.

DECEMBER: EVENING OR EVEN YEARS

DATE (FEAST DAY)	PSALMS	FIRST LESSON	SECOND LESSON
1	80	Isa 44	Luke 9:18-50
2	83	Isa 45	Luke 9:51-end
3	85	Isa 46	Luke 10:1-24
4	88	Isa 47	Luke 10:25-end
5	89:19-52	Isa 48	Luke 11:1-28
6	91	Isa 49	Luke 11:29-end
7	94	Isa 50	Luke 12:1-34
8	97, 98	Isa 51	Luke 12:35-53
9	102	Isa 52	Luke 12:54—13:9
10	104	Isa 53	Luke 13:10-end
11	105:25-45	Isa 54	Luke 14:1-24
12	106:19-48	Isa 55	Luke 14:25—15:10
13	107:23-43	Isa 56	Luke 15:11-end
14	109	Isa 57	Luke 16
15	113, 114	Isa 58	Luke 17:1-19
16	116, 117	Isa 59	Luke 17:20-end
17	119:25-48	Isa 60	Luke 18:1-30
18	119:73-88	Isa 61	Luke 18:31—19:10
19	119:105-128	Isa 62	Luke 19:11-28
20	119:153-176	Isa 63	Luke 19:29-end
21 (Thomas)	120, 121	Isa 64	Luke 20:1-26
22	124, 125, 126	Isa 65	Luke 20:27—21:4
23	129, 130, 131	Isa 66	Luke 21:5-end
24 (Christmas Eve)	134, 135	Song of Songs 1	Luke 22:1-38
25 (Christmas)	85, 110	Song of Songs 2	Luke 2:1-14
26 (Stephen)	137, 138	Song of Songs 3	Luke 22:39-53
27 (John)	141, 142	Song of Songs 4	Luke 22:54-end
28 (Innocents)	143	Song of Songs 5	Luke 23:1-25
29	145	Song of Songs 6	Luke:23:26-49
30	147	Song of Songs 7	Luke 23:50—24:12
31	149, 150	Song of Songs 8	Luke 24:13-end

† *Indicates a portion which may be read optionally instead of the whole chapter*

Psalter

DATE	MORNING PSALMS	EVENING PSALMS
1	1, 2, 3, 4, 5	6, 7, 8
2	9, 10, 11	12, 13, 14
3	15, 16, 17	18
4	19, 20, 21	22, 23
5	24, 25, 26	27, 28, 29
6	30, 31	32, 33, 34
7	35, 36	37
8	38, 39, 40	41, 42, 43
9	44, 45, 46	47, 48, 49
10	50, 51, 52	53, 54, 55
11	56, 57, 58	59, 60, 61
12	62, 63, 64	65, 66, 67
13	68	69, 70
14	71, 72	73, 74
15	75, 76, 77	78
16	79, 80, 81	82, 83, 84, 85
17	86, 87, 88	89
18	90, 91, 92	93, 94
19	95, 96, 97	98, 99, 100, 101
20	102, 103	104
21	105	106
22	107	108, 109
23	110, 111, 112, 113	114, 115
24	116, 117, 118	119:1-32
25	119:33-72	119:73-104
26	119:105-144	119:145-176
27	120, 121, 122, 123, 124, 125	126, 127, 128, 129, 130, 131
28	132, 133, 134, 135	136, 137, 138
29	139, 140	141, 142, 143
30	144, 145, 146	147, 148, 149, 150
31	148	Ecc 3:14-22

If there is a 31st day of the month, psalms are chosen from among the Songs of Ascents (120 to 134).

Readings for Holy Days Whose Dates Vary

Ash Wednesday
Psalm: 38
First Lesson: Isa 58:1-12
Second Lesson: Luke 18:9-14
Collect: Page 91

Maundy Thursday
Psalm: 41
First Lesson: Daniel 9
Second Lesson: John 13:1-20
Collect: Page 93

Good Friday
Psalm: 40
First Lesson: Lam 3:1-36
Second Lesson: John 18
Collect: Page 93

Holy Saturday
Psalm: 88
First Lesson: Lam 3:37-58
Second Lesson: Heb 4
Collect: Page 93

Easter
Psalm: 118
First Lesson: Exod 15
Second Lesson: Acts 2:22-32
Collect: Page 93

Ascension
Psalms: 8, 47
First Lesson: 2 Kings 2
Second Lesson: Eph 4:1-17
Collect: Page 94

Pentecost
Psalm: 48
First Lesson: Isa 11
Second Lesson: John 16:1-15
Collect: Page 94

Collects   An appendix containing collects for these and other Holy Days—those marked in the lectionary and on this page and also all of Holy Week—can be found on page 90.

Collects for Holy Days

These collects may be prayed instead of the daily collects in the Daily Office. Here they are sorted approximately by chronological order, including prayers for several national holidays along with the holy days, but some have fixed dates and others move with Easter or the days of the week.

The Circumcision and Holy Name of Jesus Christ (1 Jan)
Eternal Father, you gave to your incarnate Son the holy name of Jesus to be the sign of our salvation: Plant in every heart, we pray, the love of him who is the Savior of the world, our Lord Jesus Christ; who lives and reigns with you and the Holy Spirit, one God, in glory everlasting. Amen.

The Epiphany: The Manifestation of Christ to the Gentiles (6 Jan)
O God, by the leading of a star you manifested your only Son to the peoples of the earth: Lead us, who know you now by faith, to your presence, where we may see your glory face to face; through Jesus Christ our Lord, who lives and reigns with you and the Holy Spirit, one God, now and for ever. Amen.

Baptism of Our Lord (10 Jan)
Father in heaven, who at the baptism of Jesus in the River Jordan proclaimed him your beloved Son and anointed him with the Holy Spirit: Grant that all who are baptized into his Name may keep the covenant they have made, and

boldly confess him as Lord and Savior; who with you and the Holy Spirit lives and reigns, one God, in glory everlasting. Amen.

***Confession of St Peter** (18 Jan)*
Almighty Father, who inspired Simon Peter, first among the apostles, to confess Jesus as Messiah and Son of the living God: Keep your Church steadfast upon the rock of this faith, so that in unity and peace we may proclaim the one truth and follow the one Lord, our Savior Jesus Christ; who lives and reigns with you and the Holy Spirit, one God, now and for ever. Amen.

***Conversion of St Paul** (25 Jan)*
O God, by the preaching of your apostle Paul you have caused the light of the Gospel to shine throughout the world: Grant, we pray, that we, having his wonderful conversion in remembrance, may show ourselves thankful to you by following his holy teaching; through Jesus Christ our Lord, who lives and reigns with you, in the unity of the Holy Spirit, one God, now and for ever. Amen.

***The Presentation of Christ in the Temple** (2 Feb)*
Almighty and everliving God, we humbly pray that, as your only-begotten Son was this day presented in the temple, so we may be presented to you with pure and clean hearts by Jesus Christ our Lord; who lives and reigns with you and the Holy Spirit, one God, now and for ever. Amen.

***St Matthias** (24 Feb)*
Almighty God, who in the place of Judas chose your faithful servant Matthias to be numbered among the Twelve: Grant that your Church, being delivered from false apostles, may always be guided and governed by faithful and true pastors; through Jesus Christ our Lord, who lives and reigns with you, in the unity of the Holy Spirit, one God, now and for ever. Amen.

Ash Wednesday
Almighty and everlasting God, you hate nothing you have made and forgive the sins of all who are penitent: Create and make in us new and contrite hearts, that we, worthily lamenting our sins and acknowledging our wretchedness, may obtain of you, the God of all mercy, perfect remission and

forgiveness; through Jesus Christ our Lord, who lives and reigns with you and the Holy Spirit, one God, for ever and ever. Amen.

St Joseph (19 Mar)
O God, who from the family of your servant David raised up Joseph to be the guardian of your incarnate Son and the spouse of his virgin mother: Give us grace to imitate his uprightness of life and his obedience to your commands; through Jesus Christ our Lord, who lives and reigns with you and the Holy Spirit, one God, for ever and ever. Amen.

The Annunciation (25 Mar)
Pour your grace into our hearts, O Lord, that we who have known the incarnation of your Son Jesus Christ, announced by an angel to the Virgin Mary, may by his cross and passion be brought to the glory of his resurrection; who lives and reigns with you, in the unity of the Holy Spirit, one God, now and for ever. Amen.

Palm Sunday
Almighty and everliving God, in your tender love for the human race you sent your Son our Savior Jesus Christ to take upon him our nature, and to suffer death upon the cross, giving us the example of his great humility: Mercifully grant that we may walk in the way of his suffering, and also share in his resurrection; through Jesus Christ our Lord, who lives and reigns with you and the Holy Spirit, one God, for ever and ever. Amen.

Monday of Holy Week
Almighty God, whose most dear Son went not up to joy but first he suffered pain, and entered not into glory before he was crucified: Mercifully grant that we, walking in the way of the cross, may find it none other than the way of life and peace; through Jesus Christ your Son our Lord, who lives and reigns with you and the Holy Spirit, one God, for ever and ever. Amen.

Tuesday of Holy Week
O God, by the passion of your blessed Son you made an instrument of shameful death to be for us the means of life: Grant us so to glory in the cross of Christ, that we may gladly suffer shame and loss for the sake of your Son our Savior Jesus Christ; who lives and reigns with you and the Holy Spirit, one God, for ever and ever. Amen.

Wednesday of Holy Week

Lord God, whose blessed Son our Savior gave his body to be whipped and his face to be spit upon: Give us grace to accept joyfully the sufferings of the present time, confident of the glory that shall be revealed; through Jesus Christ your Son our Lord, who lives and reigns with you and the Holy Spirit, one God, for ever and ever. Amen.

Maundy Thursday

Almighty Father, whose dear Son, on the night before he suffered, instituted the Sacrament of his Body and Blood: Mercifully grant that we may receive it thankfully in remembrance of Jesus Christ our Lord, who in these holy mysteries gives us a pledge of eternal life; and who now lives and reigns with you and the Holy Spirit, one God, for ever and ever. Amen.

Good Friday

Almighty God, we pray you graciously to behold this your family, for whom our Lord Jesus Christ was willing to be betrayed, and given into the hands of sinners, and to suffer death upon the cross; who now lives and reigns with you and the Holy Spirit, one God, for ever and ever. Amen.

Holy Saturday

O God, Creator of heaven and earth: Grant that, as the crucified body of your dear Son was laid in the tomb and rested on this holy Sabbath, so we may await with him the coming of the third day, and rise with him to newness of life; who now lives and reigns with you and the Holy Spirit, one God, for ever and ever. Amen.

Easter Day

Almighty God, who through your only-begotten Son Jesus Christ overcame death and opened to us the gate of everlasting life: Grant that we, who celebrate with joy the day of the Lord's resurrection, may be raised from the death of sin by your life-giving Spirit; through Jesus Christ our Lord, who lives and reigns with you and the Holy Spirit, one God, now and for ever. Amen.

St Mark (25 Apr)

Almighty God, by the hand of Mark the evangelist you have given to your Church the Gospel of Jesus Christ the Son of God: We thank you for this witness, and pray that we may be firmly grounded in its truth; through Jesus Christ our Lord, who lives and reigns with you and the Holy Spirit, one God, for ever and ever. Amen.

***S*TS *P*HILIP *& J*AMES (*1 M*AY)**
Almighty God, who gave to your apostles Philip and James grace and strength to bear witness to the truth: Grant that we, being mindful of their victory of faith, may glorify in life and death the Name of our Lord Jesus Christ; who lives and reigns with you and the Holy Spirit, one God, now and for ever. Amen.

***A*SCENSION *D*AY**
Almighty God, whose blessed Son our Savior Jesus Christ ascended far above all heavens that he might fill all things: Mercifully give us faith to perceive that, according to his promise, he abides with his Church on earth, even to the end of the ages; through Jesus Christ our Lord, who lives and reigns with you and the Holy Spirit, one God, in glory everlasting. Amen.

***T*HE *V*ISITATION (*31 M*AY)**
Father in heaven, by your grace the virgin mother of your incarnate Son was blessed in bearing him, but still more blessed in keeping your word: Grant us who honor the exaltation of her lowliness to follow the example of her devotion to your will; through Jesus Christ our Lord, who lives and reigns with you and the Holy Spirit, one God, for ever and ever. Amen.

***D*AY OF *P*ENTECOST (*W*HITSUNDAY)**
Almighty God, on this day you opened the way of eternal life to every race and nation by the promised gift of your Holy Spirit: Shed abroad this gift throughout the world by the preaching of the Gospel, that it may reach to the ends of the earth; through Jesus Christ our Lord, who lives and reigns with you, in the unity of the Holy Spirit, one God, for ever and ever. Amen.

***T*RINITY *S*UNDAY (*S*UN. AFTER *P*ENTECOST)**
Almighty and everlasting God, you have given to us your servants grace, by the confession of a true faith, to acknowledge the glory of the eternal Trinity, and in the power of your divine Majesty to worship the Unity: Keep us steadfast in this faith and worship, and bring us at last to see you in your one and eternal glory, O Father; who with the Son and the Holy Spirit live and reign, one God, for ever and ever. Amen.

St Barnabas (11 Jun)
Grant, O God, that we may follow the example of your faithful servant Barnabas, who, seeking not his own renown but the well-being of your Church, gave generously of his life and substance for the relief of the poor and the spread of the Gospel; through Jesus Christ our Lord, who lives and reigns with you and the Holy Spirit, one God, for ever and ever. Amen.

Nativity of St John the Baptist (24 Jun)
Almighty God, by whose providence your servant John the Baptist was wonderfully born, and sent to prepare the way of your Son our Savior by preaching repentance: Make us so to follow his teaching and holy life, that we may truly repent according to his preaching; and, following his example, constantly speak the truth, boldly rebuke vice, and patiently suffer for the truth's sake; through Jesus Christ your Son our Lord, who lives and reigns with you and the Holy Spirit, one God, for ever and ever. Amen.

Sts Peter & Paul (29 Jun)
Almighty God, whose blessed apostles Peter and Paul glorified you by their martyrdom: Grant that your Church, instructed by their teaching and example, and knit together in unity by your Spirit, may ever stand firm upon the one foundation, which is Jesus Christ our Lord; who lives and reigns with you, in the unity of the Holy Spirit, one God, now and for ever. Amen.

Independence Day (4 Jul)
Lord God Almighty, in whose Name the founders of this country won liberty for themselves and for us, and lit the torch of freedom for nations then unborn: Grant that we and all the people of this land may have grace to maintain our liberties in righteousness and peace; through Jesus Christ our Lord, who lives and reigns with you and the Holy Spirit, one God, for ever and ever. Amen.

St Mary Magdalene (22 Jul)
Almighty God, whose blessed Son restored Mary Magdalene to health of body and of mind, and called her to be a witness of his resurrection: Mercifully grant that by your grace we may be healed from all our infirmities and know you in the power of his unending life; who with you and the Holy Spirit lives and reigns, one God, now and for ever. Amen.

***St James, Son of Zebedee** (25 Jul)*
O gracious God, we remember before you today your servant and apostle James, first among the Twelve to suffer martyrdom for the Name of Jesus Christ; and we pray that you will pour out upon the leaders of your Church that spirit of self-denying service by which alone they may have true authority among your people; through Jesus Christ our Lord, who lives and reigns with you and the Holy Spirit, one God, now and for ever. Amen.

***The Transfiguration** (6 Aug)*
O God, who on the holy mount revealed to chosen witnesses your well-beloved Son, wonderfully transfigured, in raiment white and glistening: Mercifully grant that we, being delivered from the disquietude of this world, may by faith behold the King in his beauty; who with you, O Father, and you, O Holy Spirit, lives and reigns, one God, for ever and ever. Amen.

***St Mary the Virgin** (15 Aug)*
O God, you have taken to yourself the blessed Virgin Mary, mother of your incarnate Son: Grant that we, who have been redeemed by his blood, may share with her the glory of your eternal kingdom; through Jesus Christ our Lord, who lives and reigns with you, in the unity of the Holy Spirit, one God, now and for ever. Amen.

***St Bartholemew** (24 Aug)*
Almighty and everlasting God, who gave to your apostle Bartholomew grace truly to believe and to preach your Word: Grant that your Church may love what he believed and preach what he taught; through Jesus Christ our Lord, who lives and reigns with you and the Holy Spirit, one God, for ever and ever. Amen.

***Holy Cross Day** (14 Sep)*
Almighty God, whose Son our Savior Jesus Christ was lifted high upon the cross that he might draw the whole world to himself: Mercifully grant that we, who glory in the mystery of our redemption, may have grace to take up our cross and follow him; who lives and reigns with you and the Holy Spirit, one God, in glory everlasting. Amen.

***St Matthew** (21 Sep)*
We thank you, heavenly Father, for the witness of your apostle and evangelist Matthew to the Gospel of your Son our Savior; and we

pray that, after his example, we may with ready wills and hearts obey the calling of our Lord to follow him; through Jesus Christ our Lord, who lives and reigns with you and the Holy Spirit, one God, now and for ever. Amen.

Holy Michael and All Angels (29 Sep)

Everlasting God, you have ordained and constituted in a wonderful order the ministries of angels and mortals: Mercifully grant that, as your holy angels always serve and worship you in heaven, so by your appointment they may help and defend us here on earth; through Jesus Christ our Lord, who lives and reigns with you and the Holy Spirit, one God, for ever and ever. Amen.

St Luke (18 Oct)

Almighty God, who inspired your servant Luke the physician to set forth in the Gospel the love and healing power of your Son: Graciously continue in your Church this love and power to heal, to the praise and glory of your Name; through Jesus Christ our Lord, who lives and reigns with you, in the unity of the Holy Spirit, one God, now and for ever. Amen.

St James of Jerusalem, Brother of Jesus (23 Oct)

Grant, O God, that, following the example of your servant James the Just, brother of our Lord, your Church may give itself continually to prayer and to the reconciliation of all who are at variance and enmity; through Jesus Christ our Lord, who lives and reigns with you and the Holy Spirit, one God, now and for ever. Amen.

Sts Simon and Jude (28 Oct)

O God, we thank you for the glorious company of the apostles, and especially on this day for Simon and Jude; and we pray that, as they were faithful and zealous in their mission, so we may with ardent devotion make known the love and mercy of our Lord and Savior Jesus Christ; who lives and reigns with you and the Holy Spirit, one God, for ever and ever. Amen.

All Saints' Day (1 Nov)

Almighty God, you have knit together your elect in one communion and fellowship in the mystical body of your Son Christ our Lord: Give us grace so to follow your blessed saints in all virtuous and godly living, that we may come to those ineffable joys that you have prepared for those who truly love you; through Jesus Christ our Lord, who with you and the Holy Spirit lives and reigns, one God, in glory everlasting. Amen.

Christ the King (Last Sunday before Advent)
Almighty and everlasting God, whose will it is to restore all things in your well-beloved Son, the King of kings and Lord of lords: Mercifully grant that the peoples of the earth, divided and enslaved by sin, may be freed and brought together under his most gracious rule; who lives and reigns with you and the Holy Spirit, one God, now and for ever. Amen.

Thanksgiving Day
Almighty and gracious Father, we give you thanks for the fruits of the earth in their season and for the labors of those who harvest them. Make us, we pray, faithful stewards of your great bounty, for the provision of our necessities and the relief of all who are in need, to the glory of your Name; through Jesus Christ our Lord, who lives and reigns with you and the Holy Spirit, one God, now and for ever. Amen.

Saint Andrew (30 Nov)
Almighty God, who gave such grace to your apostle Andrew that he readily obeyed the call of your Son Jesus Christ, and brought his brother with him: Give us, who are called by your holy Word, grace to follow him without delay, and to bring those near to us into his gracious presence; who lives and reigns with you and the Holy Spirit, one God, now and for ever. Amen.

The First Sunday in Advent
Almighty God, give us grace to cast away the works of darkness, and put on the armor of light, now in the time of this mortal life in which your Son Jesus Christ came to visit us in great humility; that in the last day, when he shall come again in his glorious majesty to judge both the living and the dead, we may rise to the life immortal; through him who lives and reigns with you and the Holy Spirit, one God, now and for ever. Amen.

The Second Sunday in Advent
Merciful God, who sent your messengers the prophets to preach repentance and prepare the way for our salvation: Give us grace to heed their warnings and forsake

our sins, that we may greet with joy the coming of Jesus Christ our Redeemer; who lives and reigns with you and the Holy Spirit, one God, now and for ever. Amen.

The Third Sunday in Advent
Stir up your power, O Lord, and with great might come among us; and, because we are sorely hindered by our sins, let your bountiful grace and mercy speedily help and deliver us; through Jesus Christ our Lord, to whom, with you and the Holy Spirit, be honor and glory, now and for ever. Amen.

The Fourth Sunday in Advent
Purify our conscience, Almighty God, by your daily visitation, that your Son Jesus Christ, at his coming, may find in us a mansion prepared for himself; who lives and reigns with you, in the unity of the Holy Spirit, one God, now and for ever. Amen.

Saint Thomas (21 Dec)
Everliving God, who strengthened your apostle Thomas with firm and certain faith in your Son's resurrection: Grant us so perfectly and without doubt to believe in Jesus Christ, our Lord and our God, that our faith may never be found wanting in your sight; through him who lives and reigns with you and the Holy Spirit, one God, now and for ever. Amen.

Christmas Eve (24 Dec)
O God, you have caused this holy night to shine with the brightness of the true Light: Grant that we, who have known the mystery of that Light on earth, may also enjoy him perfectly in heaven; where with you and the Holy Spirit he lives and reigns, one God, in glory everlasting. Amen.

Christmas Day (25 Dec)
Almighty God, you have given your only-begotten Son to take our nature upon him, and to be born [this day] of a pure virgin: Grant that we, who have been born again and made your children by adoption and grace, may daily be renewed by your Holy Spirit; through our Lord Jesus Christ, to whom with you and the same Spirit be honor and glory, now and for ever. Amen.

Saint Stephen (26 Dec)
We give you thanks, O Lord of glory, for the example of the first martyr Stephen, who looked up to heaven and prayed for his

persecutors to your Son Jesus
Christ, who stands at your right
hand; where he lives and reigns
with you and the Holy Spirit, one
God, in glory everlasting. Amen.

Saint John the Evangelist (27 Dec)

Shed upon your Church, O Lord,
the brightness of your light, that
we, being illumined by the teaching
of your apostle and evangelist
John, may so walk in the light of
your truth, that at length we may
attain to the fullness of eternal life;
through Jesus Christ our Lord, who
lives and reigns with you and the
Holy Spirit, one God, for ever and
ever. Amen.

The Holy Innocents (28 Dec)

We remember today, O God, the
slaughter of the holy innocents
of Bethlehem by King Herod.
Receive, we pray, into the arms of
your mercy all innocent victims;
and by your great might frustrate
the designs of evil tyrants and
establish your rule of justice, love,
and peace; through Jesus Christ
our Lord, who lives and reigns with
you, in the unity of the Holy Spirit,
one God, for ever and ever. Amen.

LENTEN PRAISE

DURING LENT, PRAY THIS INSTEAD OF THE TE DEUM DURING THE MORNING OFFICE (PAGE 15)

PRAY THE BENEDICTUS ES.

1979 Book of Common Prayer

Glory to you, Lord God of our fathers; you are worthy of praise; glory to you.

Glory to you for the radiance of your holy Name; we will praise you and highly exalt you for ever.

Glory to you in the splendor of your temple; on the throne of your majesty, glory to you.

Glory to you, seated between the Cherubim; we will praise you and highly exalt you for ever.

Glory to you, beholding the depths; in the high vault of heaven, glory to you.

Glory to you, Father, Son, and Holy Spirit; we will praise you and highly exalt you for ever.

Made in United States
Troutdale, OR
07/13/2024